SpringerBriefs in Psych

MW00803118

Behavioral Criminology

Series editor

Vincent B. Van Hasselt, Fort Lauderdale, FL, USA

More information about this series at http://www.springer.com/series/10850

David L. Shapiro • Charles Golden • Sara Ferguson

Retrying Leopold and Loeb

A Neuropsychological Perspective

 Springer

David L. Shapiro
College of Psychology
Nova Southeastern University Center
for Psychological Studies
Fort Lauderdale, FL, USA

Charles Golden
Nova Southeastern University
Fort Lauderdale, FL, USA

Sara Ferguson
Nova Southeastern University
Fort Lauderdale, FL, USA

ISSN 2192-8363   ISSN 2192-8371   (electronic)
SpringerBriefs in Psychology
ISSN 2194-1866   ISSN 2194-1874 (electronic)
SpringerBriefs in Behavioral Criminology
ISBN 978-3-319-74599-2   ISBN 978-3-319-74600-5   (eBook)
https://doi.org/10.1007/978-3-319-74600-5

Library of Congress Control Number: 2018932339

Printed on acid-free paper

This Springer imprint is published by the registered company Springer International Publishing AG part of Springer Nature.
The registered company address is: Gewerbestrasse 11, 6330 Cham, Switzerland

Preface

They called it the "Crime of the Century." Two brilliant young men, Nathan Leopold and Richard Loeb, both from very affluent families in Chicago, kidnapped a 14-year-old boy, killed him, and demanded a $10,000 ransom for what they described as "the thrill of it." They were convinced that it was the "perfect crime." In fact, one of the motivations for the offense was the belief that they were so clever they could outwit the police in their investigation. They were wrong. The piece of evidence most helpful in bringing about their arrest was the discovery of a pair of glasses at the crime scene that belonged to Nathan Leopold. The glasses apparently had a very unusual frame and only three existed in the city of Chicago at that time.

Fort Lauderdale, FL, USA

David L. Shapiro
Charles Golden
Sara Ferguson

Contents

Chapter 1
The Crime

A worker at the American Maize Products Company, having just finished his night shift at the factory, was walking near a railroad crossing that ran across a culvert just over the Indiana line from Illinois. He looked down at the culvert and was shocked by what he saw. He went down an embankment and saw what he thought might have been a person who had drowned with feet protruding from the culvert. He yelled and waved to some railroad workers who were approaching in two gasoline-powered handcars. They joined the first man, pulled a limp body from the pipe, and placed it on dry land. They had hoped that the person might still be alive, but after they turned the body over, it was clear that it was that of a young boy, naked and dead. The workers obtained a tarpaulin, put the body in it, and carried it up to the handcar. One of the men, looking around trying to piece together what had happened, noticed a pair of eyeglasses on the ground. He picked them up, but did not mention the glasses to the other workers. He could not tell if the glasses belonged to the boy or to someone else. When the police came, he gave the glasses to the police.

Several miles to the north, a mailman delivered a letter to the home of a man by the name of Jacob Franks. Jacob Franks' son, Bobby, had not returned from school that day. Franks and his wife were, of course, very concerned. When he read the note, it reinforced his worst fears that his 14-year-old son had been kidnapped. The note stated that Franks' son had been kidnapped, but that he was well and safe (in fact, he was already dead). The note said that no harm would come to the boy if Mr. Franks followed certain instructions regarding a $10,000 ransom. Franks was told not to contact the police. He was told that further instructions would follow. It was signed by "George Johnson." Franks received a subsequent phone call instructing him to take a taxi from his home to a pharmacy where he would get further instructions. Mr. Franks, by that time, knew that his son was dead, so he did not take the money to the drug store.

The investigation proceeded very rapidly with several people being under suspicion. Among them was a teacher at the Harvard School where young Bobby Franks had been a student. This teacher was described as being "too friendly" with some of the male students, and was being questioned by the police. The body of Bobby Franks had been burned by hydrochloric acid on both the face and genitals, and for

© Springer International Publishing AG 2018

D. L. Shapiro et al., *Retrying Leopold and Loeb*, SpringerBriefs in Psychology, https://doi.org/10.1007/978-3-319-74600-5_1

that reason the police suspected that the crime might have involved some kind of sexual perversion.

The teachers at the Harvard School were suspects for two reasons: They had access to the boys, and they knew that Jacob Franks was wealthy and able to afford a $10,000 ransom. Because the ransom note was flawlessly written, the police thought that only an educated person could have composed it. A typewriter expert said that the ransom note was typed by someone unfamiliar with touch typing since the pressure on the various keys used was different. Also, teachers were paid very little, less than $2000 a year, and the $10,000 ransom would be equivalent to 5 years' salary. Walter Wilson, the mathematics teacher, showed an unusual interest in the Franks children several months earlier. He had taken Bobby Franks and his younger brother, Jacob, on an excursion and had not returned with the boys until 1 o'clock in the morning. Suspicion raged whether Wilson was a pedophile. He was single, had no girlfriend, and told the police he did not know any young ladies around Chicago. Two other teachers, Richard Williams, the athletics coach, and Mott Mitchell, the English teacher, were also held in police custody. The detectives had searched Williams' apartment and found four bottles of brown-colored liquid, which, according to the police, might correspond to the copper colored stains on Bobby's face. William said it was merely a liniment that he used to rub on the athletes. Mitchell had a semi-annual mortgage payment due the day of the kidnapping and this also made the police suspicious. The mortgage on the house was exactly $10,000. Both of these teachers were beaten by the police. There was also speculation about whether Bobby had been sexually molested. The medical examiner claimed that he had not been victimized sexually, but, in his final report, hinted that someone may have raped the boy; he noted that, "the rectum was dilated and would admit easily one middle finger."

At the same time, the police had discovered that the glasses noted above, belonged to a young man by the name of Nathan Leopold whose family lived in the same affluent area of Chicago as the Franks family. When questioned, Nathan Leopold said that he frequently went to the area where the body was found because he was very interested in ornithology and that there were many different species of birds there. He contended that the glasses might have fallen out of his pocket when he tripped while bird-watching. The prosecuting attorney asked him to fall deliberately to see if the glasses fell out of his pocket. They did not. Eventually, when he picked the coat up, the glasses did fall out.

When asked where he was that day, Leopold initially stated that he could not remember. He later told a story upon which he and Loeb had previously agreed. The story was that they had had lunch, bought some alcohol, got intoxicated, and later picked up some girls. The girls were, according to the story, unwilling to have sexual relations with Nathan and Richard, so they drove the girls' home. The police interrogated Nathan Leopold for several hours and then began to question Loeb as well.

For some reason, Loeb's story differed from Leopold's in that he told police that he had had lunch with Leopold, but that Leopold subsequently dropped him off at his home, making no mention of their story of picking up some girls. Both boys also maintained that they were driving around in Nathan Leopold's bright red car.

When the police questioned the chauffeur at the Leopold home, he told the police that Nathan had asked him to fix the brakes on his red car on that same day. The police believed that this was a break in the case since they now had two major inconsistencies. In fact, Leopold and Loeb had designed an elaborate scheme in which Leopold, using the name Morton Ballard, rented a car and it was this rented car that they used during the crime.

The police continued to interrogate Leopold and Loeb, confronting them with the inconsistencies in their stories, as well as the statement of Sven Englund, the chauffeur who was sure that he was repairing the brakes on Nathan's car at the time. Nathan maintained that he and Loeb were out driving around in that same car. Mr. Englund also recalled that Nathan and Richard had been washing out the interior of the car after they returned home. When he asked what they were doing, they indicated that they had been drinking and spilled some wine in the car.

Another thing that made the State's Attorney suspicious was that upon searching of Nathan Leopold's room they had found correspondence between him and Richard Loeb suggesting the two of them may have had a romantic relationship. For that reason, when Leopold and Loeb both talked to Mr. Crowe and to the police about having picked up some girls that evening, it appeared to Mr. Crowe that it was a bit suspicious. Mr. Crowe also believed that Leopold and Loeb were involved in the crime since Leopold's handwriting matched that on the envelope enclosing the ransom letter addressed to Jacob Franks.

The eyeglasses, of course, had been found near the corpse and Leopold and Loeb had concocted an alibi that could not be confirmed. Detectives had discovered typed legal notes belonging to Leopold that matched the typed ransom note delivered to Jacob Franks the day after the murder. Of course, there were, in addition, the inconsistent stories about using Nathan's automobile, while the chauffeur said he was repairing the brakes on that same car.

The prosecutor confronted Leopold with the entire narrative provided by Loeb and when Leopold said that was just a prosecutor's trick, the prosecutor presented information that was accurate and that only Loeb could have known. They both eventually confessed, although each maintained that it was the other who hit Bobby Franks with a chisel.

The police later took Leopold and Loeb to the area where they had disposed of the body. As they were driving to the scene of the crime, one of the police officers asked Nathan how he felt about the killing. Nathan said it did not concern him since he had no moral beliefs and religion meant nothing to him. Serving one's own needs was the best guide to conduct. In this case, his was an intellectual participation in the killing, like the desire of a scientist to perform an experiment. The killing was an experiment, nothing more. Nathan wanted to experience the sensation of murdering another human being. It was that simple.

Initially, Leopold was perceived as the more evil of the two due to his total absence of affect and was viewed as insensitive to anyone else's suffering. Loeb was perceived as the one who followed Leopold's wishes. Loeb was garrulous, charming, and spoke on a wide variety of topics quite easily.

It was only later, as the true nature of their personalities emerged, that both seemed equally culpable; Leopold because of a bizarre delusion allegedly based on the writings of Nietzsche and Loeb who had a desire to be seen as the most brilliant criminal in the history of Chicago.

The crime was so unfathomable and inflamed the populace so much that the prosecuting attorney decided to seek the death penalty, an unusual move since no one as young as the defendants (Loeb was 18 and Leopold was 19) had ever been executed in Cook County. The prosecutor, Robert Crowe, stated to the press that he had a "hanging case" and that he was willing to submit it to a jury the very next day.

The families of the defendants hired the brilliant criminal defense attorney Clarence Darrow to defend their sons. Darrow was an avowed foe of capital punishment. He stated several years later in his autobiography, *The Story of My Life*, that even when there is the possibility of capital punishment, "I went in to do what I could for sanity and humanity against the wave of hatred and malice that, as ever, was masquerading under its usual nom de plume: 'Justice'" (Darrow & Dershowitz, 1996).

Darrow was also a staunch believer in the developing field of psychiatry which posited at that time that all behavior was the product of unconscious forces that we do not understand, and could only be fathomed by intensive psychoanalytic examination and treatment. Darrow's philosophy was a mechanistic one, that personality and behavior were determined by birth and environment, and that there was no such thing as "free will". Therefore, no one could be considered responsible for his or her actions. To that end, Darrow retained the services of several well-known, distinguished psychiatrists and one psychologist who would testify that both Leopold and Loeb were mentally ill. However, none of these experts was able to state that either Leopold or Loeb did not "know the difference between right and wrong" (the standard for insanity in Illinois at that time). Nor could they specify the causal relationship between the mental illness and the crime. The contention that the defendants were mentally ill, but not legally insane, resulted in a great deal of legal haggling since the prosecutor insisted that Darrow was trying to get insanity in through a "back door". When it became clear that Darrow was hiring mental health experts, the assumption was that he would pursue a defense of Not Guilty by Reason of Insanity.

In a surprise move on the first day of trial, Darrow withdrew the pleas of not guilty made by the defendants at their arraignment and pled his defendants guilty of the crimes charged. He sought to enter expert testimony as a possible mitigating factor, which, along with their youth, might spare them from the death penalty. A guilty plea would result in there being no trial and, therefore, no jury. The judge alone would be responsible for evaluating the testimony and sentencing the defendants. Darrow knew that the judge in this case, John Caverley, had a reputation as a liberal and intelligent jurist. Extensive expert testimony then followed from both the defense and the prosecution. Darrow's closing argument, interestingly enough, made only passing reference to the mental health issues and focused on his indictment of the death penalty. Some later stated that Darrow put the death penalty on trial.

Ultimately, the judge sentenced both Leopold and Loeb to "Life plus 99 years." He also paid scant attention to the issues of mental illness raised in the expert testimony and focused on the issue of their youth and, as Darrow had so eloquently argued, the fact that no one that young had ever been executed in Cook County, Illinois.

Darrow was a brilliant orator, but presented himself as a country bumpkin. A fascinating description of Darrow came from the journalist Ben Hecht, who, many years later in a book entitled *Gaily, Gaily*, stated "The picture of Darrow drawling in front of a jury box was a notable scene. The great barrister artfully gotten up in baggy pants, frayed linen, and string tie, and 'playing dumb' for the jury as if he were no lawyer at all, but a cracker-barrel philosopher groping for a bit of human truth" (Hecht, 1966).

Both Leopold and Loeb were sentenced to prison. Loeb was killed by another inmate in 1936. Leopold organized the prison library, taught, and even volunteered for some potentially life-threatening trials of certain medications, and was eventually paroled in 1958. He moved to Puerto Rico, married, and continued teaching until his death in 1971.

The crime and subsequent trial both sickened and fascinated the general public for many years. Several non-fiction books were written, most notably by Hal Higdon (*Leopold and Loeb: The Crime of the Century*) and by Simon Baatz (*For the Thrill of it*). It also was described in fiction in a novel entitled *Compulsion* by Meyer Levin, which appeared in 1956. This was subsequently made into a movie by the same name in 1959. Another movie called "Rope" (Hitchcock, 1948) was loosely based on the case, as well as a recent play entitled "Thrill Me".

One of the reasons that the case continues to fascinate people is that the crime is still incomprehensible, at least in terms of what we knew about human behavior in the 1920s. Much of the expert testimony was, as noted earlier, based on the theories of Sigmund Freud, which at that time were in their infancy. Even in reading the expert testimony, the question of how Leopold and Loeb's childhood histories led to the horrific crime of killing for the thrill of it is unclear. That is, the reports focused on the childhood seduction of Leopold, a preoccupation on his part with the Crucifixion and Loeb's learning to steal and lie in order to escape the wrath of his governess. There did not appear to be any causal nexus between what were perhaps abnormal childhoods and the kidnapping and killing of a 14-year-old boy.

One of the more elaborate psychoanalytic explanations for the crime is found in the novel *Compulsion*. Here, the character known in the book as "Willie" goes to Vienna to study with Freud. Many years later, he tells Sid Silver (the young man that represents Meyer Levin) about his theory that the crime represented a masturbatory fantasy since the murder weapon was a chisel wrapped in tape and that stuffing the body into the culvert was a symbolic "return to the womb." This character "Willie" also posits that the pouring of hydrochloric acid on the boy's body, especially his genital area was an expression of castration anxiety. The use of acid was explained during the trial as an attempt to conceal the victim's identity, having nothing to do with sexual concerns. However, even if we accept this psychoanalytic reconstruction, it still does not answer the matter of the causal connection between the theory and the crime (Levin, 1956).

The question then is what could have resulted in two brilliant, though obviously mentally disturbed young men, to commit this crime? While we may never know all the answers to this question, a large body of research in brain-behavior relationships has developed in recent years. One of the experts in the trial testified to some neurological abnormalities in Leopold's brain structure, but the significance of this remained unclear. What we will attempt to do in this brief volume is to look at the facts of the crime, the expert testimony, and the recent research regarding brain-behavior relationships to determine if these neurological findings shed any more light on this crime. One of the more fascinating observations made by several of the experts in their testimony was that neither Leopold nor Loeb would have, by themselves, committed such a crime. It was the unique, and at times unusual, interplay between the psychotic beliefs of Leopold and the psychopathy of Loeb that led to the crime. It was in a particularly tragic manner "a perfect storm".

Shocking as the crime was, in a sense, it was the natural outgrowth of an interaction between Nathan Leopold and Richard Loeb that began several years earlier. It bore the earmarks of not only a very unusual interaction between them, but also pathological distortions of several philosophical constructs.

Nathan Leopold was born on November 19, 1904, in Chicago. His family had emigrated from Germany. Leopold was a child prodigy who reportedly spoke a few words at the age of 4 months and scored very high on intelligence tests. He went to some very prestigious private schools and, at the time of the murder at age 19, had already completed a Bachelor's Degree at the University of Chicago and was planning to enter Harvard Law School in the fall. He spoke five languages and apparently was familiar with a number of others. He also had developed a reputation as an ornithologist and with several others had already published a book on a very rare species of bird.

Richard Loeb was born on June 11, 1905 in Chicago. His family, like the Leopolds, was very well-to-do and in fact his father was a retired Vice President of Sears Roebuck and Company and a well-known attorney. Loeb, like Leopold, was very intelligent. He attended the University of Michigan in Ann Arbor, Michigan and was the youngest student ever to graduate from that school at the age of 17. Despite his brilliance, he was also described as lazy and unmotivated. From an early age, he became fascinated by crime and spent much of his spare time reading detective novels.

Both boys grew up in an affluent section of Chicago near the University of Chicago. They knew each other on a casual basis but their relationship intensified and solidified at the University of Chicago. They found out that each had a fascination with crime, though from different perspectives.

In Loeb's fantasy life, he was the "master criminal" someone who could commit high profile crimes and continually outwit the police. Leopold, on the other hand, developed a fascination with the German philosopher, Friedrich Nietzsche, especially his concept of the "uebermensch" (overman, or as sometimes loosely translated, superman). A few words are needed about this concept since Leopold, based on his own psychological needs, perverted Nietzsche's ideas. According to Nietzsche in *Thus Spoke Zarathustra*, the book in which he introduced the concept of the "uebermensch," the overman is an individual who is willing to risk everything in order to make humanity better. He contrasts this with the concept of the "last man" who is able to think of only his own comfort. An uebermensch, then, has his own values that can influence the lives of others in the direction of improving the lot of humanity. These ideas can dominate and enhance the lives of others even though others may be unaware of the influence. The uebermensch can affect history indefinitely by entering people's minds and directing their thoughts, dominating the thoughts of others in a creative manner (Nietzsche & Kaufmann, 1995).

Nietzsche also defended the importance of emotions, seeing them as natural and seeing their suppression as psychologically destructive. He attacked religion for inhibiting emotion and impulse. He regarded this suppression as a thwarting of human nature. He regarded a world without passion and emotion as unnatural. This uebermensch represents an individual that can transcend the traditions that bind together much of society. However, as noted above, this is seen as an aspect of creatively enhancing society for the better (Nietzsche & Kaufmann, 1995).

As we know, Nazi Germany distorted the concept of the uebermensch to justify destroying people who were not regarded as members of the master race. In a similar manner, although on an individual, as opposed to a societal basis, Nathan Leopold distorted the Nietzschean concept to justify his own needs. He believed that he was one of these superior individuals and, therefore, was not bound by the ethics and rules of society. He regarded himself as exempt from societal laws and, as a result, not liable for anything he does. Leopold also decried the influence of emotion, believing that emotions were misleading. He strove to be a person who based his life on pure intellect. Therefore, we see in his interpretation of Nietzsche two major distortions: Leopold saw his being a superman as freeing him from any of the laws of society including harming others. This is not found anywhere in Nietzsche's writings. In fact, the uebermensch is seen as someone who influences society in a positive direction. Leopold's suppression of emotions is also inconsistent with Nietzsche's emphasis on the importance of emotion. A good example of this absence of affect is found in Leopold's conversations with the police when showing them the route he and Loeb had taken on the day of the offense, telling them that he had no feelings, that the crime was pure intellect, a scientific experiment.

It was with this series of distorted ideas along with Loeb's fantasy of being a master criminal that the crime was set in motion. In fact, Leopold and Loeb started off their lives of crime with petty thefts, vandalism, and at least one arson. They broke into a fraternity house at the University of Michigan and stole, among other items, the typewriter on which they eventually typed the ransom note. Loeb's motivation included wanting public recognition for the cleverness of his crimes, as well as admiration for his daring. On one occasion, he and Leopold stole a car. Apparently, the owner saw them and began chasing them. Loeb then jumped out of the moving car. Presumably, so did Leopold, although this is unclear. After not receiving the recognition and media coverage desired, Loeb convinced Leopold that they needed to plan and execute a "perfect crime" that would be sensational, gain public attention, and since they believed they would not be caught, would confirm their beliefs in themselves as "supermen" above the law. Leopold had apparently gotten Loeb to incorporate the superman notion into his need to be the master criminal.

They decided that kidnapping and murder of a young boy would be their perfect crime. Meticulous planning, over the course of 7 months went into the crime, all the way from how they would abduct the child to where they would dispose of the body. To detract attention from the true nature of their crime, they planned to make it look like a kidnapping with a demand for ransom, when, in fact, their victim would already be dead. The plan was very complicated with several sets of instructions delivered to the victim's family one at a time by phone and the final demand typed with a location for a money drop specified. They searched for a victim and eventually settled on 14-year-old Bobby Franks, who lived nearby and was actually Loeb's second cousin. It was this meticulous and careful planning that the prosecution used to demonstrate just how aware of the wrongfulness of their behavior Leopold and Loeb were.

On May 21, 1924, using an automobile that Leopold had rented under an assumed name, they offered Bobby Franks a ride home from school. Bobby initially refused, but eventually came into the car because Loeb said he wanted to tell him about one of his tennis rackets (Loeb had played tennis with his cousin Bobby on previous occasions). While there was some dispute over who struck the fatal blow, most evidence suggested that Loeb, who was sitting in the back seat, did so while Leopold drove. Loeb struck the Franks boy with a chisel in the head, dragged him into the back seat and gagged him. Bobby died soon thereafter. They then drove to a location which they had previously selected, about 25 miles south of Chicago just over the Indiana line. Leopold was familiar with the area as he had been involved in bird watching in the area. Leopold and Loeb waited until dark, removed and discarded the victim's clothes and concealed the body in a culvert under some railroad tracks. They poured hydrochloric acid on the face, on an abdominal scar, and on his genital area to conceal his identity and the fact that he was circumcised.

News spread rapidly and, by the time Leopold and Loeb returned to Chicago, word had spread that Bobby Franks was missing. The two men then called Mrs. Franks, with Leopold telling her he was "George Johnson," that he had kidnapped the boy and that ransom instructions would follow. They then mailed the typed ransom note, burned their clothing, and attempted to wash the bloodstains from the rental car. The ransom note arrived the following morning and Leopold called a second time delivering instructions for payment of the ransom. However, before any ransom money was delivered, the body was discovered, exposing the kidnapping scheme. They disposed of the typewriter and burned a robe in which they had concealed the body.

In searching near the culvert, police found a pair of glasses that had a very unusual hinge mechanism on the frame purchased by only three customers in the Chicago area. The police quickly eliminated two of the people and the third was Nathan Leopold. He told the police that they may have dropped out of his pocket during a bird watching trip. The police asked him what pocket he would carry glasses in and, when he replied, they requested he demonstrate how the glasses might have fallen out. He was unable to do so.

Leopold and Loeb were formally questioned on May 29th. They both agreed to tell the police a pre-arranged story that that they had picked up two women and, after driving around, dropped them off. As noted earlier, Loeb merely stated that Leopold dropped him off and made no reference to picking up the women. They said they were in Leopold's car. This was exposed as a lie, because Leopold's chauffeur told police that he was repairing Leopold's car the same day that the two men said they were using it. The chauffeur's wife verified that the car was in the garage that night. Leopold and Loeb insisted that the chauffeur must have been wrong in his recollections.

Shortly thereafter, both confessed, although each blamed the other for the fatal blow, insisting he just did the driving. Both spoke of the fact that they did it for the "thrill", their belief that they were "supermen" and that they believed they were committing the "perfect crime." Leopold, demonstrating the isolation of affect noted above, stated to his attorney, "It is just as easy to justify such a death as to justify an entomologist killing a beetle on a pin." For him, it was an experiment, an intellectual exercise.

As evidence of the lack of affect, immediately after the crime, they drove around waiting for nightfall to dispose of the body. They begin driving along country roads looking for a place to eat. They stopped at a roadside convenience store with large billboards on it and Leopold returned to the car with a couple of hot dogs and two bottles of root beer.

Leopold said that a thirst for knowledge was highly commendable and, in fact, should always be a priority. It did not matter if pursuit of this knowledge resulted in extreme pain or injury to others. He further compared it to a 6-year-old boy pulling the wings off of a fly, if by so doing he learns that without wings the fly is helpless.

When asked if they made arrangements to divide the money, Loeb indicated that they were going to split it evenly. He said money entered into it some way, but the main thing was the adventure of it. Leopold, in a similar manner, said that it was a pure love of the excitement, of doing something different and the satisfaction and ego of putting something over on others.

As noted above, Loeb viewed himself as the "master criminal." He felt that he could deceive the police by cleverly discussing with them his theories surrounding the crime and the police would not recognize that they were actually talking to a killer. This, of course, is consistent with the thrill-seeking noted earlier. In fact, Loeb told one detective, "If I were to murder anyone, it would be just such a cocky little son of a bitch as Bobby Franks." Such a narcissistic belief in his own powers of deception are quite remarkable, but totally consistent with his fantasy life.

Some of Loeb's statements to the police reveal a great deal about his personality and desire to be the master criminal. He stated to one of the officers that this thing (the murder) will be the making of him. He believed that he would spend a few years in jail, be released, come out to a new life, work hard, amount to something, and have a career. He stated that the crime did not bother him that much and that he only had one or two thoughts about it. What did bother him was that it interfered with his relationship with his mother and that he was a disgrace to the family. Several weeks thereafter Loeb commented that he should feel sorry that he killed Bobby Franks, but he did not feel it and did not have any feeling about it from the very start. He stated that that was why he could do it. He observed that there was nothing stopping him. He stated that he was sorry about his family but not as much as he should be.

When asked about the ransom note, Leopold observed that the letter was "better than average", concise and well-phrased, instilling terror and impelling action. Once again, he emphasized the quality of the letter and its ability to frighten people with a total absence of any personal emotion. He did not speak of the fact that the note stated that the Franks boy was still alive, when in fact he was already dead. He further seemed proud of the crime, discussing how he and Loeb had rehearsed the kidnapping three times with all its details specified. The only thing lacking was the identity of the boy they were going to kidnap and kill. Perhaps most disturbing was his statement to the police that it was an experiment, just as easy as an entomologist impaling an insect on a pin.

Several weeks later, Leopold stated that since he would probably be executed, he wanted to determine if there was an afterlife. He decided to compose ten riddles and have a group of scientists try to communicate with him after death to see if he had been able to solve the riddles. He also decided that he would write a book because it would be an excellent opportunity to make his views more widely known and because of the public's interest in the case; nowhere is there any recognition of the pain he is inflicting on others.

While the State emphasized and tried to make the ransom of $10,000 a motive for the offense, it was clear that Richard grew more excited from outlining the idea for the perfect crime. He told Nathan that they should kidnap a child and to increase the intricacy of the crime they should demand a ransom from the child's parents. The money was important, not for its own sake, but to magnify the complexity of the crime. They had to leave instructions to obtain the ransom while making sure they left no clues for the police. They would have to kill the child because it would be foolish if the victim could identify them later.

Prosecutor Crowe wanted to have the defendants examined by psychiatrists before the defense had an opportunity to do so. In fact, Crowe set up the examinations at a time that Darrow and the defense team were trying to interview the defendants. This would not be allowed in present legal settings since the prosecution can only hire rebuttal mental health experts once the defense had made a proffer of a mental health defense. In fact, in one highly publicized United State Supreme Court case in 1980, Estelle v. Smith, one of the reasons for the High Court reversing and remanding was that the prosecution, with no notice to the defense, had sent in a psychiatrist to the jail to allegedly examine a defendant for competency, when, in fact, the purpose of the examination was to elicit an opinion to be presented at the capital sentencing procedure.

Crowe had the defendants examined by three psychiatrists in a group setting along with several members of the prosecution team and several police officers. Once again, such a group interview would be prohibited nowadays. Prosecutor Crowe retained the services of Doctor Hugh Patrick, a Professor Emeritus from Northwestern University Medical School, Doctor Archibald Church, a Professor in that same medical school, and Doctor William Krohn, a psychiatrist in private practice. All three, unlike the experts that Darrow would call, could best be described as traditional, not following the new theories of unconscious motivation promulgated by Freud and his followers. They believed rather that mental illness and insanity were caused by intellectual impairment and their focus was on the conscious rather than the unconscious mind. Doctor Patrick referred to psychoanalysis as "corkscrewing" and stated that psychoanalytic methods were unnecessary and could be harmful.

Leopold was examined first and looked at the interview as an opportunity to demonstrate his intellect. He engaged one of the doctors in a debate about the merits of intelligence testing, maintaining that the mind was too complex to be measured. Loeb was subsequently brought in and questioned while Leopold was present. Loeb insisted that Leopold was the more intelligent of the two of them, implying that he was dominated by Leopold, attempting to undercut the belief that Loeb had been the mastermind. This interview was then followed by a brief physical examination.

In fact, the entire psychiatric examination by the doctors retained by Crowe was brief and done in a group setting, a fact that Darrow would later explore on cross-examination of the prosecution experts. Darrow asked each doctor whether it was typical for them to see their patients, even those in a legal setting, in a group with prosecutors and police officers present. Of course, all of the doctors agreed that it was atypical, as was the brevity of their examination.

All three psychiatrists agreed that neither Nathan nor Richard had shown even the slightest signs of mental illness and, to the contrary, that they had been self-possessed, coherent, rational, and lucid with no evidence of insanity.

The State's Attorney did have a dilemma because he was trying to establish the fact that Leopold and Loeb were legally sane. At the same time, he wondered whether he could get a jury to believe that kidnapping a 14-yearold boy solely for the thrill of the experience was not evidence of insanity. This appeared to be the reason why at the trial Mr. Crowe, the prosecutor, made little mention of the "thrill of killing" and rather painted the picture of the money being the motive for the murder.

When the State's Attorney invited the prosecution's psychiatrists to examine Leopold and Loeb, he knew that it would be difficult for them to claim temporary insanity since they had meticulously planned the murder for 6 months, paying close attention to detail—from arranging to collect the ransom while avoiding capture, establishing a false identity, purchasing the necessary items, carefully hiding the corpse, disposing of Bobby's clothing and cleaning the rental car. It was an ugly crime. The murder was neither an impulsive act nor a crime of passion. Some states allowed an insanity defense based on "irresistible impulse", but Illinois followed the McNaughten rule which stated that a person was not criminally responsible if they could not appreciate the nature and quality or the wrongfulness of their acts and made no reference to irresistible impulse.

During a psychiatric examination, both Leopold and Loeb demonstrated that they knew that murder was wrong and, in fact, admitted that they could distinguish right from wrong. Doctor Church asked Nathan Leopold, "When you made this plan to do the killing, you understood perfectly your responsibilities in this matter" and Leopold answered in the affirmative. He also asked Leopold about his knowledge of the consequences of a criminal act such as murder and again Leopold answered, Yes. He did admit that demonstrating their superiority over the Chicago police was a motive though. Leopold felt that that was more the basis of Loeb's and a small part of his.

Loeb also stated he knew the difference between right and wrong. When asked if he felt that he had done the wrong thing in this killing, whether he knew that it was wrong to kidnap the boy and whether he knew the consequences of the act, Loeb answered all in the affirmative. Doctor Krohn asked whether they had any feeling of retracting or giving up the scheme and Loeb stated that he did not think so. Loeb also admitted in response to questioning by the doctor that he did not want to be called a quitter. He hated anybody that was a coward. He had the power to refrain from doing it. He could have refrained from doing the wrong thing. He answered yes to, "You had the power of will and choice to decide whether you would do it or not." These questions were designed to elicit opinions about whether or not the commission of the crime was a compulsion, even though technically such testimony would not be admissible, since it had to do with "irresistible impulse", an insanity standard which, as noted above, did not exist in Illinois at that time. While it would not be legally admissible, defense expert testimony could attempt to "slip it in" while discussing other matters. Walter Bachrach, one of Darrow's co-counsel, did, in fact, in his remarks speak of compulsions and the 1956 novel based on the case was entitled, *Compulsion* (Levin, 1956).

Chapter 2
The Trial/Hearing

As noted earlier, Richard Loeb's father hired the eloquent and brilliant criminal defense attorney, Clarence Darrow to represent his son. Nathan Leopold was represented by attorneys Benjamin and Walter Bachrach. They all worked together during the trial. Darrow had a reputation of taking on cases that most others believed could not be won, yet Darrow managed to have success on many occasions. Darrow was fervent in his opposition to the death penalty and had saved many defendants from execution in the past. In this case, State's Attorney Robert Crowe announced that he intended to pursue the death penalty. Darrow and Crowe had been adversaries in a number of previous cases so there was no love lost between the two. Darrow's task was twofold then: To oppose Crowe, who had been smarting from some of the previous cases where Darrow had bested him; and, to denounce the death penalty, which Crowe insisted that this case merited. Some of their verbal exchanges are instructive. Crowe described Darrow as the "distinguished gentleman whose profession it is to protect murder in Cook County". Darrow, on the other hand, stated that Crowe had done everything possible to elevate the notoriety of the murder, portraying it as the worst such act in the history of Illinois. "I have heard," stated Darrow, "nothing but the cry for blood. I have heard raised from the office of the State's Attorney nothing but the breath of hate!"

Darrow and Bachrach entered a not guilty plea on the part of their clients, Leopold and Loeb, and broadly hinted that their defense would involve the mental state of the defendants, although they never actually entered a plea of not guilty by reason of insanity. Shortly before the trial, Darrow and Bachrach met along with the fathers of the defendants. Darrow shared his belief that such a plea would mean there would be a jury trial. Darrow was of the opinion that a jury would not accept such a defense, which would result in a finding of guilt and a recommendation for the imposition of the death penalty. Therefore, he recommended withdrawing the plea of not guilty, pleading the clients guilty and attempting to use the expert testimony of a number of psychiatrists to establish evidence of mitigation. If accepted, it could result in a sentence of life imprisonment. The other advantage to the guilty plea was that it could be argued in front of the Judge only, who would solely be responsible for the sentence. As noted

© Springer International Publishing AG 2018
D. L. Shapiro et al., *Retrying Leopold and Loeb*, SpringerBriefs in Psychology,
https://doi.org/10.1007/978-3-319-74600-5_2

earlier, Judge John Caverly had a reputation as a liberal judge. In a capital trial (one in which there is the possibility of a sentence of death), the prosecutor argues what are called "aggravating circumstances" (those that would make the crime appear more heinous and cruel, such as killing a child, a major issue in this case, or killing a police officer). The defense will argue "mitigating circumstances" (those that would diminish the seriousness of the crime, such as the fact that a defendant acted under duress, was a juvenile, or that he or she suffered from a mental illness which impaired their behavioral controls). The jury is supposed to weigh aggravators against mitigators. If aggravators outweigh mitigators, the sentence is death. If mitigators outweigh aggravators, the sentence would be life imprisonment. Of course, in the real world, this weighing of factors is subject to many influences, including the arousal of jurors' emotions.

On the opening day of the trial, Darrow announced that he was entering a plea of guilty and using expert testimony of the psychiatrists to build a case for mitigation. When State's Attorney Crowe angrily accused the defense of trying to get insanity in through the back door, Walter Bachrach explained the difference between a defendant suffering from a mental illness, which is a medical or psychological condition—and from which the defense believed both defendants suffered—and insanity, which was a legal construct having to do with mental illness leading to an inability to tell the difference between right and wrong at the time of the offense. Both Leopold and Loeb, through their answers to interview questions by doctors hired both by defense and prosecution, clearly knew the wrongfulness of their actions. However, the defense would argue that the mental illnesses led to a compulsion to commit the crime (even though, as noted earlier, such testimony would technically not be admissible). Darrow, in fact, was very skillful, talking about the mental illness of Leopold and Loeb, but never actually relating these illnesses causally to the crime. In his comments to Judge Caverly at the time, it was announced that they would plead the defendants guilty and seek to enter their mental illness as mitigation along with their youth, Benjamin Bachrach said, "What we desire to do is to determine the degree of mental responsibility of the defendants." This is essentially an argument for the concept of diminished mental capacity, one which did not exist in Illinois at that time; the defendants, according to the law, were either insane or they were not, with no partial responsibility.

When Doctor William A. White was called to the witness stand by the defense, Crowe immediately objected before White testified. Crowe said that Doctor White would try to argue that Leopold and Loeb were mentally ill. Equating mental illness with insanity, he stated that they could not plead guilty and simultaneously offer an insanity defense.

Indeed, in American law, this was not formalized until 1972 in the American Law Institute Model Penal Code, which spoke of diminished capacity as an inability to form the requisite specific intent to commit the offense. The State's Attorney Mr. Crowe indicated that, "The defense is not permitted to introduce any insanity testimony because the law states that a plea of guilty to a fact automatically presumes the defendant to be sane" and, for the defense to attempt to introduce psychiatrists to testify regarding the mental condition of Leopold and Loeb "would be going clearly outside the rules of evidence… There can be no insanity for a person who pleads guilty… There is but one punishment which will satisfy the prosecution… and we will demand they be hanged."

In his July 31, 1924 reply, Walter Bachrach said, "Now, I wish at this time to emphasize the difference between a mental disorder or mental disease, and insanity. Now there are certain forms of mental disorder; there are certain forms of mental diseases that do not constitute insanity... Epilepsy is a form of mental disease which does not constitute a defense to a charge of murder or any other crime... [W]e have other forms of mental illness such as deliria melancholia and mental defects of various kinds all of which constitute mental disorder and mental disease which fall far short of constituting insanity."

Darrow and Bachrach called several well-known psychiatrists to testify about the mental illnesses of Leopold and Loeb. Some of the features noted were very similar in the two defendants, while some were quite discrepant. Some of the doctors focused more on the personal history of psychopathology while others looked at the presence of any physical abnormalities.

2.1 Evaluation of the Defendants by Karl Bowman and Harold Hulbert

The first doctors to see Leopold and Loeb for the defense were Doctor Karl Bowman, Chief Medical Officer of the Boston Psychopathic Hospital, and Doctor Harold Hulbert, a neuropsychiatrist in private practice who would be assisting him. Bowman believed that questions regarding mental health and mental illness lay in the field of endocrinology. It was believed by Bowman and others who shared this orientation that mental illness could be eliminated if researchers could understand the effects of hormones on the body. Such scientists would look, for instance, at such structures as the thyroid, pituitary, and pineal glands, all of which manifested themselves through deviations in the urine, blood, pulse, blood pressure, and metabolism. Darrow, himself a determinist who rejected the notion of free will, believed that human behavior was totally determined by environmental stimuli acting on the body that resulted in certain specified and measurable outcomes. The focus of the Bowman-Hulbert report was on the physical findings. This was supplemented by a detailed life history, the events of the crime itself, and the details of the relationship between Leopold and Loeb, including their sexual contacts with one another.

Nathan Leopold told the psychiatrist that there had been two experiences which profoundly affected his philosophy of life. One was the death of his mother, whom he regarded very highly. Leopold decided if she had to suffer so much in the world, then God must be cruel and Leopold refused to worship Him. He also stated that to be intellectually honest, he tried to cut out emotions and that his ideas must be based on cold-blooded intellect. He, therefore, developed a mechanical theory of the universe, which he saw as a mass of electrons and the human mind only a complicated center of reflexes. Of importance to this case was that he saw no difference between right and wrong and felt that justice had no objective status. He believed that the only wrong he could do was to make a mistake and that happiness was the only thing in life that mattered to him.

Doctors Hulbert and Bowman discussed Nathan Leopold's sex life as well. He apparently had never been attracted to women and looked on them as intellectually inferior. Recall that there had been the earlier occurrence of his being seduced by his governess.

Around the age of 10, he and two friends formed a club which had some initiation ceremonies which involved masturbation and homosexual behavior. Later on, when he met Richard Loeb, there was apparently mutual masturbation.

The reports further noted that he and Loeb would drive around and pick up women, attempting to have sexual relationships, but on several occasions Leopold found himself impotent. He felt that his desire toward women was primarily an intellectual one and he merely went with women because it was the right thing to do.

When questioned about his sex life, Richard Loeb denied that he had ever masturbated and that his governess had carefully avoided any discussion about sexuality. It was only when he entered college (recall he entered college at age 14) did he learn that people had sexual intercourse. The first time he attempted to have intercourse, he contracted a venereal disease and had to undergo 9 months of treatment.

Loeb's sex drive was described as low, with his stating that he could get along easily without it, and that the actual act of sex was unimportant to him. Other times during the interviews, he bragged about the frequency of his sexual relationships with women, so this was apparently an area of some degree of concern for him. Of course, Loeb was a habitual liar, which, as we have noted, is quite consistent with his psychopathic tendencies. He was apparently a very skillful liar and he could lie without any fluctuation at all in his appearance. He would make false claims, at times mislead and would often omit certain facts. While he stated abstractly that it was wrong to lie, his own lies brought him no sense of guilt. He concealed many things even from his brother, including having robbed him on several occasions.

Regarding Leopold's truthfulness, the psychiatrists noted that while he seemed fairly open during the examination, on a number of occasions he would present rather plausible lies.

Leopold's willingness to cooperate with Richard Loeb came, according to the psychiatrists, from his feelings of low self-esteem, which also caused him a feeling of sexual inferiority. He had a marked sex drive, but was unable to satisfy it in heterosexual relations and this was profoundly upsetting for him. Leopold also was unathletic, feeling physically inferior to others, and unable to cooperate with others in a physical manner. Therefore, as noted before, he tried to compensate for this by a world of fantasy in which his desire for physical perfection would be satisfied, notably in a master-slave fantasy. Here he, as the slave is the strongest man in the world, would fight as a champion for his side against the strongest man on the other side and would always win. These fantasies began around the age of 5 when he began idolizing his older brother, who was in military school.

When he was 12 years of age, Leopold went to a summer camp and was attracted to a counselor, who was approximately age 18.

Loeb had an equally active fantasy life beginning at age 10, where he imagined himself able to withstand the impact of bullets and fantasized himself as an ideal man, very good-looking, athletic and rich, owning multiple automobiles and also being a football hero. He would also picture himself in jail being stripped of his clothing, shoved around, and whipped. He described this punishment as pleasant. This fantasy evolved into that of his being a criminal mastermind and he generally saw himself involved in a variety of criminal activities. He derived intense pleasure from these fantasies of being a master criminal. He felt superior to others, in that they did not know he was connected with the crime while he knew the truth about it. In fact, a number of his actual crimes tended to repeat this very theme. The centrality of his being the criminal mastermind occurred on many occasions, with Loeb feeling that he could escape detection from the greatest detectives of the world and that he could work out a plan for a crime that would stir the country and never be solved. He was always the leader in these fantasies though he had a number of associates. He did not believe that he should be in an organized gang, and he did not plan to use his legal training to further a career in crime; nor did he want to use his studies to assist him in criminal activities.

It is noteworthy, and one of the reasons that we have called this a "perfect storm," that Loeb's criminal fantasies of being a mastermind and Leopold's fantasies of being a powerful slave serving a mighty king, eventually fused together. The result, of course, was the death of Bobby Franks.

Loeb's metabolic rate was a −17% which was described as unusually low, pointing to possible glandular or endocrine dysfunction. His blood tests revealed him to be slightly anemic. Skull x-rays revealed no evidence of intracranial pressure, and no obvious abnormalities. Cranial nerves were normal. There was a slightly elevated blood nitrogen of 37 (normal is 25–35). Sella turcica was normal as were anterior, middle and posterior skull fossae. Blood pressure was 100/65 and his pulse rate was 88–92 which was described as "below normal".

Leopold's metabolic rate was a −5%, slightly low, but not distinctly abnormal. Blood pressure, like Loeb's, was low, and there was evidence that he did not metabolize sugar properly. While Loeb's skull x-rays were essentially within normal limits, Leopold's demonstrated some evidence of pathology. Some of the suture lines in the skull were obliterated and there was evidence of osteosclerosis. There was a hardening of the cartilage in the brain usually seen in ages 30–45, not in a 19-year-old like Leopold. The inner surface of the skull showed many depressions. The right coronal suture showed osteosclerosis throughout the greater part of its length. In the parieto-occipital areas, the lamboidal suture was less well visualized than expected for a 19-year-old. There were markings on the middle branches of the middle meningeal and some congestion and crowding of the pituitary gland. There was further evidence of hyperpituitarism, diseased sex glands, and, overall, a pathological union of various bones in the skull. The premature hardening and calcification of the pineal gland was associated with premature mental development, shallow mood, thick dry skin, coarse hair, and low body temperature. There were premonitory signs of kidney disease (family history of same) and, in childhood, a very low resistance to disease. He had what doctors described as a "peculiar and aberrant form of chicken pox," in which he had a pronounced fever but no rash, followed by a second attack of measles and a mild form of scarlet fever manifested by sweating, weakness, and fainting. There were also recurrent skin infections and a disorder of the adrenal medulla. His depressed pulse rate, respiration, temperature, and blood pressure were seen as possible signs of Bright's disease. Until the age of 9, he had recurrent gastrointestinal distress, fever, headaches, vomiting, vasomotor instability, and frontal and occipital headaches (especially with the fevers). Also noted in the physical examination was facial asymmetry, prominent eyes, and dermographia, a disorder of the nervous control of the blood vessels.

Loeb had started his criminal career at about age 8 or 9. At that time, he stole money from a boy in the neighborhood, hiding it under the roof of a playhouse in his back yard. Of note, according to the report, there was the total absence of guilt or fear, a feature which, of course, was evident in descriptions of the killing of Bobby Franks. In fact, Loeb was described as elated over the feeling that not only had he stolen the money, but that the rightful owner did not know where it was, while he, Loeb, of course did. This is another theme that is reported at the time of the crime. Loeb would talk with people about the crime, listen to their theories and challenge them, all the time feeling so superior that he knew about the crime while others did not. Around the same age, Loeb and a friend opened a lemonade stand. On one occasion, Loeb stole the cash register and buried it, again experiencing the thrill of knowing where the money was while others did not. His motive appeared consistently to be the thrill rather than the actual taking of the money. He also stole liquor from relatives and committed some minor thefts. When Loeb was about 15 years of age, he met Leopold who had also committed petty thefts as a young boy. He had stolen stamps from another boy's collection and stolen some ties from his older brother. He demonstrated no embarrassment in describing these thefts, though they did not seem to provide the same "high" for him as they did for Loeb. Leopold and Loeb developed a scheme for cheating at bridge, as well as committing several acts of petty thievery together. They also had their first homosexual encounter at that time. While Leopold was attracted to Loeb, Loeb saw Leopold as an accomplice in the thefts and the sexual contact was, apparently, for Loeb not as invested with feeling as it was for Leopold. It was also at this time that they stole a car, were chased, and then jumped from the moving car. They later disguised themselves and went to the scene of the car wreck. Loeb again experienced the thrill of knowing something that others did not know. Subsequently, they stole another car, parked it and went to eat in a restaurant. When the police questioned the patrons of the restaurant, they denied knowing anything about it. Once again, we see the dynamics of outwitting the police. Loeb also described the thrill of several other times when they threw bricks through the windows of cars and stores, being pursued by the car's occupants or the police. Loeb described these as memorable.

Loeb hoped that these crimes would attract publicity and was often disappointed when he would read the newspapers and find no mention of the crimes. He and Leopold would also turn in false fire alarms and would remain to see the subsequent excitement. They also set several fires and would drive back to the scene with Loeb having the thrill of watching it, feeling superior to those bystanders who would guess about the cause of the fires. This fire setting was followed by several unsuccessful attempts at burglary, but Loeb still experienced the thrill of planning it carefully.

In reference to the killing of Bobby Franks, Loeb decided not to back out of the plan because he had spent so much time with Leopold planning it, not because of any concerns about killing another human being. He said, in response to a question, that he would commit the crime again if he could get the money. Leopold stated that the only reason he would not commit such a crime again was the likelihood of getting caught. Remorse or guilt had nothing to do with it. In fact, Leopold did not feel that he had done anything morally wrong, because he did not think there was such a thing as morality in the conventional sense. Rather, anything that gave him pleasure was right and wrong is something that would be unpleasant for him.

Darrow was pleased that there were some scientific findings that could bolster his assertion that Leopold and Loeb, although not legally insane, were in fact mentally ill. However, he was concerned that the jury might not understand the scientific material and, even if they did, what, if any, causal connection to the offenses could be made. In the movie "Compulsion," the District Attorney, Mr. Horne, played by E.G. Marshall, proclaims with dripping sarcasm, "so I should feel sorry for these murderers if they had a hare lip?"

Perhaps some of these connections might become more apparent in the examinations of the other psychiatrists with a more psychodynamic point of view. Doctor William Alanson White, Superintendent of St. Elizabeth's Hospital in Washington, D.C., Doctor William Healy a psychologist who administered psychological tests to Leopold and Loeb (he believed that mental defect was causally related to crime), and Doctor Bernard Glueck director of the psychiatric clinic at Sing Sing Prison, were the next to examine them.

Doctor White was well known at the American Psychiatric Association and was very involved in psychoanalytic theory. Doctor White saw both defendants on several occasions.

Doctor White spoke about the governess of Loeb, being an extremely rigid disciplinarian and critical of even the most minor infractions. She was constantly interfering with Loeb when he tried to associate with boys his own age, particularly those whom she considered less worthy than Loeb. Consistent with the earlier psychiatric report of Doctors Hulbert and Bowman, Doctor White noted that Ms. Struthers pushed him tremendously, especially in his schoolwork, was very ambitious regarding him, and pushed him further than he would have gone without that kind of backing. When Loeb finally was out on his own (that is, going to college at a young age), he basically had to grow up overnight, missing the ordinary childhood developmental experiences.

Loeb began to drink while in college in the company of young men 4–8 years older than himself and he would confide his feelings to these older boys.

Loeb also told Doctor White about the prison fantasy where he was being abused or beaten in prison. People would come and look at him in prison adoringly, especially young women. In fact, during the course of the trial, Loeb projected this image and a number of young women attempted to gain entrance to the courtroom, seemingly fascinated by Richard Loeb.

Loeb relished this role of being a celebrity in court, seeming to focus so much on this that it often got in the way of his perception that he was on trial, possibly for his life. On several occasions, there were photographs taken of Loeb making jokes, laughing, and involving Nathan Leopold in the humor, totally inappropriate in such a serious setting.

Doctor White, of course, coming from a psychoanalytic background, raised a good deal of skepticism among several members of the press. What was described as the intensity of Loeb's fantasies and peculiarities in his behavior were consistently downplayed in the media. For example, they made fun of Loeb's preoccupation even into adolescence with his teddy bear, a matter which Doctor White felt was quite important.

Regarding Leopold, Doctor White described Leopold as setting himself apart from others and that he differed from others in the direction of superiority. He described Leopold as antagonistic toward any kind of tenderness or emotions and the feelings of empathy and sympathy that average people would experience. Leopold, in fact, resented people who experienced their feelings. This led to Leopold's hedonistic philosophy, one devoted to complete and absolute selfishness with there being no place for emotions or feelings. Intelligence was the only important feature. The only crime, according to Leopold, was a mistake of intelligence. He, of course, traced this back to his preoccupation with Nietzsche and, as we have noted, greatly distorted Nietzsche's philosophy in order to justify his behavior. Doctor White also noted that Leopold used his intellectual ability to shield his feelings of inferiority, leading to a superiority and supercilious attitude. He avoided making friends, feeling that they might betray him and hurt him. Most people disliked Leopold because they thought him arrogant and conceited. The only friends he did develop were those who were attracted by his intelligence and analytical powers.

Doctor White described how Nathan began to drink and smoke at a young age and that he felt he had to excel in what other students in college did. For instance, Leopold insisted on learning languages, especially obscure ones, because he desired to be different. In reference to the Nietzsche preoccupation, he had discussed with a professor at law school the question of whether Nietzsche's superman could or could not be held responsible for their acts. In fact, under Nietzsche's philosophy, the true superman would be such a superior individual that he would not be tempted to do acts of evil.

Doctor White also described the interaction of Nathan Leopold and Richard Loeb. White described Loeb as having antisocial tendencies that increased in strength throughout the years and that he had no adequate defense mechanisms to protect him. He basically had a malignant antisocial disposition, according to Doctor White, and this fit very well with Leopold's emphasis on his uniqueness, which was merely a defense mechanism to compensate for an inferiority complex. In reference to the crime itself, Doctor White felt that the killing of Bobby Franks could be understood by seeing that Loeb needed an audience and that Nathan Leopold was his audience. He believed that Leopold did not have criminal tendencies but rather a distortion of Nietzsche's philosophy which appeared to be delusional in its extremes.

One of the defense attorneys, Mr. Bachrach, questioned Doctor White regarding the two boys' mental condition on the day of the murder. This was, of course, a difficult and potentially hazardous series of questions. We may recall that in pleading Leopold and Loeb guilty, Darrow has admitted that they did not fit the definition of legal insanity. Therefore, the testimony had to describe their mental state without suggesting that they were incapable of understanding the wrongfulness of their behavior.

Doctor White described Loeb's outstanding feature as his being infantile and that he was still a child emotionally, talking to his teddy bear. Leopold was also described as having a very primitive emotional age which Doctor White felt to be between ages 5 and 7. However, intellectually, both measured high, especially Leopold. Doctor White believed that will, intelligence, and emotions were different aspects of one unit and that one could not separate out free will.

When cross-examined, Doctor White felt that Loeb was primarily responsible for the offense, though legally it made no difference. Both boys were equally guilty under the law. Doctor White's responses to cross-examination involved admission that he had developed a close relationship with the two boys, whom he called patients. This friendliness was attacked by the prosecution as evidence of a failure to maintain objectivity. White regarded and was quoted later as saying that he found the defendants "charming."

The attorney also attacked the psychiatric testimony in the sense that none of the psychiatrists had reviewed collateral data. Therefore, none could be certain that the defendants were not lying. The defense psychiatrists, of course, talked about the consistency in the way Leopold and Loeb presented themselves as evidence that they were not lying. The State's Attorney did make an important point that, in forensic evaluations, one does need to gather collateral data and look for consistencies across data sources, a requirement that is currently regarded as standard practice in such evaluations.

The next witness, Doctor William Healy, again described the sexual relationship between Leopold and Loeb and did so in great detail.

Doctor Healy had also administered a number of intelligence tests and noted that Leopold demonstrated several examples of superior memory, such as making a list of 20 words with Leopold being able to read them precisely backward and forward. When told one word, Leopold was able to tell the preceding or following word in perfect order. Healy also stated, testing Leopold's delayed memory, that he was capable of doing this the very next day. Doctor Healy noted, however, that Leopold did very poorly on tests measuring practical reasoning, once again, highlighting the extremely rarefied and isolated aspects to Leopold's intelligence. Doctor Healy also found him, as noted earlier, extremely critical of others, condescending toward others based on his own mental attainments and very stubborn in his own opinions. Doctor Healy described him as believing that the world was wrong and that he was always right. Doctor Healy, in summary, commented about Leopold's observation that making up his mind whether or not to commit murder was about the same as making up his mind whether or not he should eat pie for dinner, the criterion being whether or not it would give him pleasure. Doctor Healy described Leopold as mentally diseased. Of course, upon cross-examination, the prosecutor asked Doctor Healy whether or not Leopold was insane. Doctor Healy avoided this question by stating that Leopold had a paranoid personality and that anything he wanted to do was right, even kidnapping and murder. He was incapable of feeling empathy, which would protect him from the disintegration of his personality. Again, there was no place for sympathy or feeling to play any part. Doctor Healy described Leopold as having a pathological personality, but had it not been for his interaction with Loeb, the crime most likely would not have occurred.

Doctor Healy described Loeb as not doing as well as Leopold on the intelligence test, having essentially only average intelligence. His language ability was poor. According to Doctor Healy, he was not interested in any mental tasks. He could work with fair attention and persistence, but he regarded it as difficult. He described Loeb as lazy, without deep interests, without apparent ambition, and seemingly incapable of completing any task. Nevertheless, Doctor Healy noted that Loeb was outgoing and well mannered. Doctor Healy described Loeb's mental condition as abnormal and stated in response to a cross-examination question, that the crime was the direct result of a diseased motivation. Once again, Doctor Healy would not respond to the issue of whether or not Loeb fit the criteria for insanity under the law. The State's Attorney on many occasions insisted that the psychiatrists were, in fact, testifying about insanity. Therefore, the State's Attorney demanded that Judge Caverly convene a jury which Judge Caverly refused to do.

The next defense witness, Doctor Bernard Glueck, described a feature noted in different ways by all of the other witnesses, namely the complete absence of any signs of normal feelings in Loeb, such as one would expect under the circumstances. Loeb evidenced no remorse, no regret and no compassion for the people involved in the situation. Doctor Glueck described an extreme discrepancy between the things that Loeb was talking about, the things he was thinking about, and the things he claimed he had carried out.

He described both Leopold and Loeb as absolutely incapable of emotionally taking in the meaning of the whole situation. He described both as suffering from a profound discord between intellect and emotion, but as noted earlier, for different reasons.

This was followed by several other witnesses, notably Doctor Hulbert, whose report we discussed earlier. Doctor Hulbert focused on the two boys' physiological abnormalities. Loeb had, according to Doctor Hulbert, an abnormally low basal metabolism, which indicated a disorder of the endocrine glands and the sympathetic nervous system. Loeb had not matured, was not normal physically or mentally, and there was a close relationship between the physical abnormalities, primarily those of the endocrine system, and his mental condition. Intellectually, he was far beyond the average boy of his age, but emotionally lagged much behind. The discrepancy between judgment and emotions, once again, was highlighted and, for this reason, based on the endocrine factors, he believed that Loeb was mentally diseased.

In describing Leopold, once again, Doctor Hulbert spoke about the fact that there was no emotion displayed. Leopold seemed only interested in getting the details correct. He appeared, according to Doctor Hulbert, to have the intellect of a man 30 years of age, but, again, had extremely impoverished emotions. He noted, once again, the judgment of a child and his sense of inferiority. He stated that the motivation for the crime was partly that of Loeb's to commit the perfect crime and a desire on Leopold's part to do whatever Loeb expected of him. Doctor Hulbert also talked about the causation of the crime as being in the interplay or interweaving of the two personalities.

The State's Attorney was sarcastic about Doctor Hulbert's testimony, stating that it was very convenient that the two had personalities which just happened to complement one another.

From the point of view of possible personality pathology, Loeb was described as immature, with only an abstract realization of what he owed to society. In other words, he could say what was expected but had no real emotional appreciation of it. Loeb felt that he did not have to inhibit his feelings, since he regarded them as minimal. Emotional reactions were like those of a 5 or 6-year old's poor judgment, with notable discrepancy between intellectual accomplishments on one end and very emotionally detached on the other end. He discussed the crime with no emotions or feelings; all psychiatric reports describe Loeb in a similar manner: a pathological disconnect between emotions and intellect and judgment. There was no capacity for remorse or grief, a dichotomy of high intellectual ability and emotional retardation. Along with this was an inability to appreciate the emotional significance of a situation. Loeb preferred to read about it in the newspapers. He had no sense of social awareness, and, therefore, no need or desire to conform to socially accepted standards. Loeb also had a need for immediate gratification. Despite his intellectual attainments, he was described as mentally lazy and unwilling to complete tasks. Words, such as glib, pathologically lying, being immodest, selfish and a skilled actor, also appear throughout these reports. He was also described as conning, manipulative, grandiose, and superficial, demonstrating what was called malignant splitting (playing one person off against another) and narcissistic. He had a very strict governess who would pit Richard against his own mother. Richard learned to be very skillful at lying to cope with this situation. The governess had no child-rearing skills and wanted Richard to be perfect, all of which resulted in increasing lying and manipulation on his part. He began stealing money at the age of 8 with no feelings of guilt, but got a thrill out of knowing where the money was while the owners did not. Killing and deceiving the authorities had the same thrill-like quality (the perfect crime) since he did not experience affect in an expected manner. At the time of the crime, Loeb was very excited about writing the ransom letter making a stir in the newspapers, having a feeling of superiority. He was described at the time of the crime as cool, self-possessed, laughing and joking. He discussed the crime publicly with satisfaction (just like earlier robberies, knowing something that others did not). He wanted to be regarded as Chicago's most intelligent criminal. The psychiatrists opined that his fantasy of criminal prowess was a compensation for feelings of inferiority. They noted that Loeb had had a head injury and concussion at age 15, but there was no attempt to relate the head injury to the offense.

Loeb suffered from mood swings when he was alone and used and manipulated his friends. While he was fearless, like going out in a boat in a storm and driving recklessly (being chased and jumping out of a moving car), this gave him a thrill, although he was physically a coward. He loved to set fires and false alarms for the thrill, watching a crowd, and knowing something they did not know. He had tremendous outbursts of energy, did not tire easily, had feelings of superiority, and always felt he was right.

In the case of Richard Loeb, then, we have a brilliant, egotistical individual, who is conning with only the capacity for superficial affect and who is manipulative and thrill seeking. It is essentially the description of what is now called a psychopath (Hare, 1991) and what Cleckley, in the 1940s, described as a "mask of sanity" (Cleckley, 1941). Of course, this examination was performed in 1924 before these concepts were well defined or delineated.

Nathan Leopold's personal history is also more detailed than that of his co-defendant, Loeb. Nathan Leopold had intense and vivid master-slave fantasies. In the fantasy, he was the very powerful, strong slave who saves his master. His master offers him freedom, but he refuses, wanting to be at one and the same time a slave, yet having the person with power be indebted to him. There was clearly sexual excitement associated with these fantasies. In fact, Loeb often assumed the role of the master in the fantasies. There was a highly structured and ritualistic sexual relationship between Leopold and Loeb with certain sexual activities, such as his placing his penis between Loeb's legs at particular times and in exchange for certain activities which he did at Loeb's behest. Violence played a central part in his sexual fantasies involving Loeb. Loeb would play the part of an intoxicated individual, who within the fantasy, is brutally attacked and sexually assaulted by Leopold. There is no indication, however, that there was any actual violence in their relationship. It was all a fantasy which was acted out. His homosexual orientation bothered Leopold a great deal and resulted in feelings of inferiority.

His method of compensation was to be cold-bloodedly intellectual, denying all feelings. Leopold was totally hedonistic and considered the needs of others only if their actions increased his feelings of pleasure. He needed immediate gratification. He seemed incapable of feelings of gratitude or of sympathy. He was quick to defend his hedonistic philosophy, seeing it as part of the Nietzschean "superman" (which, as we noted before, was his own idiosyncratic misinterpretation of the concept). Leopold regarded having a conscience as "nonsensical." His emotional detachment, the extreme dichotomy of intellectual ability with emotional retardation, and his belief that he had no duty to society, led some of the doctors to believe that he was indeed delusional. He expressed no regrets about the killing, with the exception of the fact that he got caught. Consistent with his absence of affect, he regarded murder as a small thing compared to the pleasure it gave him. Especially pleasurable for Leopold was to read about the crime in the newspapers, though he was concerned about reporters getting their facts right. He enjoyed the trial. He felt it was unique, unusual and interesting. He could learn a lot about himself and could share his hedonistic philosophy with the world. Leopold's history was remarkable for a seduction by a governess between the ages of 6 and 12, who also seduced his brother. She would bathe with both boys and Leopold would lie on her back when she was naked with her face down and insert his penis between her legs. With nothing to compare it to, Leopold assumed it was normal. This governess was followed by another who was exceedingly religious and filled Leopold's mind with many stories about the Crucifixion. Leopold developed a fascination with crucifixion and would sketch headless bodies and dissected penises. He would also kill and collect birds with no affective reaction to his behavior. From a psychodynamic point of view, of course, we have a childhood seduction followed by a fascination with sadistic and cruel punishments. He could be quite cutting verbally, sneering at the lesser intellectual abilities of others. He believed that justice had no objective existence and the only wrong was to make a mistake. He enjoyed being the center of attention and did things to impress others with his intellectual superiority. He regarded women as intellectually inferior and was arrogant and conceited about his purported superiority. Some other symptoms are suggestive of a deeper underlying mental illness. For instance, at times he would go without sleep and this would result in a state of stimulation and well being. At these times, he felt his intellectual capabilities worked more easily than usual. (Looking at this now, one has to wonder whether this represented some kind of bipolar pathology.) Finally, in his writings, Leopold indicated that when he was sick and awake at night, he would experience visual hallucinations which were vague and blurry. When driving, he would sometimes see taillights, without the presence of an automobile; he also described a number of compulsions and superstitions, constantly checking the clocks and lamps, as well as having compulsions regarding the number "3".

Several of the psychiatrists were asked whether the crime could have occurred if each defendant had acted alone; all of the doctors agreed that neither would have committed the crime by himself. This was a bizarre confluence of two brilliant young men, one of whom most likely was a psychopath and the other having an elaborate delusional system about his being a "superman" and above the laws of society. These were, of course, symptoms of mental illnesses, but not rising to the level of insanity under the law which was "not knowing the difference between right and wrong."

In cross-examining Doctor William White, Crowe decided not to fight him on psychoanalytic theory, but rather to highlight the fact that he depended only on his interviews and on one previous psychiatric report. He continually peppered Doctor White with how he knew that the defendants were telling the truth and, if they were not telling the truth, did his psychoanalysis have any value? White stated that they simply had not lied to him. Crowe pointed out that Nathan Leopold and Richard Loeb had lied on many occasions and that Doctor White did not know the details of some of the previous crimes such as fire setting. Crowe focused on the fact that White's conclusions depended entirely on what the boys had told him. This, of course, raised the whole issue of malingering, about which there were no scientific writings at the time. The first written studies appeared in the 1970s and structured validated psychological testing came later, in the 1990s.

All of the psychiatrists found a vast gulf between the defendants' emotional capacity and their intellectual ability, with both being emotionally infantile. Were this case presented today, this would clearly require a referral for a neuropsychological evaluation. The extreme disparity between emotion and intellect, the continual emphasis by the defense psychiatrist on the lack of remorse and the lack of emotion could, of course, blow up in the defense's face. This would give the grounds for the State to talk about how heinous and cruel the crime was (arguments which could be used as aggravating circumstances in a sentencing hearing).

The problem with all of the expert testimony by the defense psychiatrists was that none could describe the causal nexus between the mental illnesses—the emotionally infantile personality, the paranoia—with the crime itself.

One of the psychiatrists for the prosecution, Doctor William Krohn, testified that Loeb's faculties were in order that his hearing and eyesight were not impaired and his memory excellent. Loeb could recall every detail of the killing including the origin of the scheme 6 months before the murder. Loeb's judgment was balanced and appropriate and there were no instances when he displayed poor judgment. Krohn further stated that "[T]he stream of thought flowed without any interruption or any break from within. There was not a single remark made that was beside the point. The answer to every question was responsive." There was abundant evidence that he was perfectly oriented to time and place and his social relations. Loeb's ability to reason was entirely normal. He could group together instances and argue inductively to a logical conclusion. His attention was excellent and there was no evidence of any defect, disorder, nor lack of development or of any disease. He then described Nathan Leopold as showing no signs of neurological disease since he did not see any jerking of the limbs or an awkward unsteady gait or tremors of the body. There was no defective vision, no defective hearing; no evidence of defect of any of the sensory pathways or activities. There was no defect of the nerves leading from the brain as evidenced by gait or tremors or in the response of their pupils to light. Leopold also demonstrated no evidence of neurological disease. Krohn went on to say that there was no evidence of any organic disease of the brain and no evidence of any toxic mental condition. Leopold had a remarkable memory and could recall innumerable details of the murder. His reasoning was intact and he had been able to argue logically and coherently during the examination at the State's Attorney's office. Krohn stated that he showed remarkably close attention, that he was perfectly oriented socially as well as with reference to time and space Krohn further stated that there was nothing about the behavior or appearance of Leopold and Loeb in the courtroom to indicate mental disease such as modifications of movement that come with certain mental disorders. The defendant displayed "no slow, resisting movements that come with certain conditions known as mental disorders... [T]he gait showed freedom and ease... [T]here was no staring, no gazing fixedly, none of the positions characteristic of certain mental diseases." The other prosecution psychiatrists agreed with Krohn's conclusion that both Leopold and Loeb were free of mental disease.

Doctor Patrick found no signs of psychiatric illness and stated that there was nothing significant in the testimony presented by the defense witnesses. He asserted that the report by Doctors Bowman and Hulbert was full of inconsistencies and contradictions. For instance, he talked about the defense statement regarding the effects on the pituitary gland as being a sign of mental illness, but in reading an x-ray report, there was no report of this diminution in size. Doctor Patrick asserted that the size does not mean there was any abnormality in the pituitary gland at all. The report from Doctors Bowman and Hulbert was, according to Doctor Patrick, full of vague and meaningless statements, and that some of the statements would have been true of anyone, especially the fantasies. He noted that none of these would have compelled them to commit murder. Doctor Patrick essentially said that everyone fantasized to some extent and that Loeb's desire in his fantasies to be a master criminal did not show any abnormality, but rather that he possessed a criminal mind. He stated, "Unless we assume that every man who commits a deliberate cold-blooded murder must be by fact mentally diseased, there was no evidence of mental disease".

Doctor Church then described both Leopold and Loeb as free from mental disorder. He said that Loeb was entirely oriented, knew who he was, where he was, and the time of day. His memory was extraordinarily good. His logical powers, as manifested during the interview, were normal and there was no evidence of any mental disease. Similarly, Church said in Nathan Leopold there was no evidence of mental disease. He was perfectly oriented, had good memory, had extreme intellectual reasoning capacity, and had good judgment. The scientific findings presented by the defense according to Church had no significance and that the fantasy life of each boy contributing to a symbiosis in no way compelled the killing of Bobby Franks. Church contended the psychoanalytic evidence was insufficient grounds for mitigation of punishment. Similarly, Doctor Harold Douglas Singer observed that both defendants had been free and easy in their movements that they laughed and conversed with one another, and consulted with their attorneys in a thoughtful manner.

In Darrow's cross-examination, he heaped sarcasm on the prosecution's experts. He noted that there were 15 people in the room during the evaluation and that it was not a thorough consultation nor was it consistent with good psychiatric practice. Darrow questioned whether anyone had ever brought a patient to Doctor Church for treatment when there were that number of people present. Church agreed that he had never treated a patient or examined the patient in front of so many people. The other expert witnesses for the State, of course, had to concede that the inadequacy of the examination was the weakest link in the State's case. There had been insufficient time for the psychiatrists to properly evaluate Leopold's and Loeb's mental condition. To impeach their testimony that there was no evidence of a mental disease or defect, both Darrow and Bachrach pointed out that there were statements in the textbook authored by Krohn and Singer that discussed latent mental conditions that would not be obvious upon a brief examination.

Chapter 3
Closing Arguments

3.1 Closing Arguments for the Prosecution

The State, in its closing argument stressed the fact that the crime of Leopold and Loeb was deliberate, premeditated, and extreme. If these two defendants were not executed, according to the State, capital punishment would cease to have any meaning and should be abolished. They stressed the greatness of the turpitude, the months of planning, the alibis and false identities, the precise carrying out of every detail, the absence of impulsivity, a money motive, a kidnapping for ransom, the deliberateness of the murder, "the cruel blows of a sharp steel chisel", the gagging, the death, and the hiding of the body all took the crime out of the scale of lesser penalties and demanded the death penalty. The State contrasted Leopold and Loeb to two other defendants who had grown up in extreme poverty, in broken homes, and were illiterate and yet were sentenced to death. These two defendants, on the other hand, came from a privileged background and were well educated. The State addressed Darrow's contention that the mental conditions of these defendants should spare them from execution. The State's Attorney pointed out that Leopold and Loeb had pled guilty, therefore admitting responsibility. Responsibility for criminal acts was not divisible: a defendant either was responsible or not responsible; (partial responsibility, or what is sometimes now called diminished capacity, was not a part of the law at that time in the State of Illinois). In fact, the State argued that it was the severity of the offense, not "weak mind, fantasy, delusion, or mental disease" that should determine the punishment. Again, the State described the offense as flagrantly willful, deliberate, and premeditated, and that if the Judge, even with discretion, were to follow the law, he would have to sentence them to death. The fact that the crime was an intellectual exercise rather than a crime of passion made it especially horrifying.

Assistant State's Attorney Thomas Marshall began the opening argument for the prosecution and stated, "The position of the State is that there is but one penalty that is proportionate to the turpitude of this crime, only one penalty that applies to this

© Springer International Publishing AG 2018
D. L. Shapiro et al., *Retrying Leopold and Loeb*, SpringerBriefs in Psychology,
https://doi.org/10.1007/978-3-319-74600-5_3

crime, and that is the extreme penalty, death." Assistant State's Attorney Marshall defined turpitude as the depravity, the viciousness, the facts and the circumstances of the crime. It was noted that Leopold and Loeb thought this was funny, chuckling at the time. Marshall continued to cite cases which would be precedents for a sentence of capital punishment.

Assistant State's Attorney Joseph Savage, stated, "You have before you one of the most cold-blooded, cruel, cowardly, dastardly murders that was ever tried in the history of any court." Savage accused Leopold and Loeb of not giving Bobby Franks even a fighting chance. "The blow was struck from behind, that cowardly blow." He commented on the defense pleas for mercy and stated, "What mercy did they show to him? Why, after striking the four blows they pulled him to the rear of the car and gouged his life out. Mercy! Why, Your Honor, it is an insult in a case of this kind to come before the bar of justice and beg for mercy! I know Your Honor will be just as merciful to these two defendants sitting here as they were to Bobby Franks."

Savage continued to speak and demanded the lives of Leopold and Loeb, stating, "Hang them! Hang these heartless supermen! If we do not hang these two most brutal murderers, we might just as well abolish capital punishment because it will mean nothing in the law. And I want to say to Your Honor that the men who have reached the gallows prior to this time have been unjustly treated if these two do not follow."

The final statement from the prosecution came from the State's Attorney himself, Mr. Robert Crowe. He stated, "Before going into a discussion of the merits of the case, there is a matter I would like to refer to. The distinguished gentleman whose profession is to protect murder in Cook County and concerning whose health thieves inquire before they go to commit a crime, has seen fit to abuse the State's Attorney's Office and particularly my assistants, Mr. Marshall and Mr. Savage, for their conduct in this case. He has even objected to the State's Attorney referring to two self-confessed murderers who have pleaded guilty to two capital offenses as criminals."

> Your Honor ought not to shock their ears by such a cruel reference to the laws of this State, to the penalty of death. Why, don't you know that one of them has to shave every day of the week and that is a bad sign? The other one only has to shave twice a week and that is a bad sign. One is short and one is tall and is equally a bad sign in both of them. When they were children, they played with teddy bears. One of them has three moles on his back. One is over-developed sexually and the other not quite so good. My God, if one of them had a hare lip, I suppose Darrow would want me to apologize for having had them indicted.

> I have a right to forgive those who trespass against me as I do, in the hope that I in the hereafter will be forgiven my trespasses. As a private citizen, I have that right and as a private citizen I live that religion. But, as a public official, elected by the people, charged with the duty of enforcing the laws of my country, I have no right to forgive those who violate their country's laws.

State's Attorney Crowe went on to state that the judge had no right to forgive those who trespass against the State of Illinois, and that with the mass of evidence presented by the State, had a jury been sitting that did not return a verdict that fixed the punishment at death, every person in the community would feel that the verdict was founded in corruption.

Crowe proceeded to make demeaning remarks about the psychiatric opinions, taking on Doctor William White first. He spoke about White taking him by the hand and "led me into the nursery of two poor rich young boys, and he introduced me to a teddy bear. Then he told me some bedtime stories, and after I got through listening to them he took me into the kindergarten and presented me" to the defendants. He was then, Crowe stated, taken by the Bachrach Brothers to a psychopathic laboratory where he received a liberal education in mental disease and particularly what certain doctors did not know about them. He described the psychiatrists as "the three wise men from the east" and that they wanted to make the picture a little bit more perfect. Crowe stated that one of them was sacrilegious enough to say that "this pervert, this murderer, this kidnapper, thought he was the Christ child and that he thought his mother was the Madonna, without a syllable of evidence any place to support the blasphemous and sacrilegious statement."

Crowe then turned toward Leopold and, shaking a finger in Leopold's face, stated, "I wonder now, Nathan, whether you think there is a God or not? I wonder whether you think it is pure accident that this disciple of Nietzschean philosophy dropped his glasses or whether it was an act of Divine Providence to visit upon your miserable carcasses the wrath of God in the enforcement of the laws of the State of Illinois?" Crowe went on and stated, "I want to tell Your Honor, bearing in mind the testimony that was whispered in your ear, one of the motives in this case was the desire to satisfy unnatural lust." He stated that there was evidence of sexual abuse of Bobby Franks' body and the defense objected, indicating that there was no evidence of this. The judge sustained the objection and admonished Mr. Crowe for his attempt to bring this in. The question of sexual perversion in the killing was left unresolved. Mr. Crowe went on to state, "If the State only had half of the evidence that it did have, or a quarter of the evidence that it had, we would have had a jury in the box, and a plea of not guilty." Crowe again spoke about the defense's attempt to use the insanity defense while not calling it such. He then analyzed the Hulbert and Bowman report and noted that the report was inadequate.

Toward the end of Mr. Crowe's comments, he stated, "It is Clarence Darrow's dangerous philosophy of life" that is the real defense.

> I don't know whether Your Honor believes that officer (who had testified as to what the defendants had told him) or not, but I want to tell you, if you have observed these two defendants during the trial, if you have observed the conduct of their attorneys and their families... everyone connected with the case have laughed and sneered and jeered...

3.2   Closing Arguments for the Defense

The defense, having three attorneys, the Bachrach brothers and Darrow, was allowed to present two closing arguments. Walter Bachrach went first. He began by noting that the law gives the judge discretion to take into account the condition of a murderer in sentencing, and that should include mental condition as well. Bachrach skillfully wove together the youth of the defendants with their mental illnesses, indicating that both could not totally comprehend the effect of their actions on others and that both lacked experience in social awareness, social relations, and understanding of moral behavior. Bachrach stressed that the psychiatric testimony was not an attempt to evade responsibility, but rather to suggest that mental condition should be used as a mitigating factor in deciding the punishment. There was no doubt, Bachrach continued that both defendants were mentally ill. Nathan Leopold suffered from a paranoid psychosis (what we would now call a delusional disorder). While cognitions were intact, Leopold had delusions of grandeur (the superman belief), self-satisfied superiority, disregard of others, and exaggerated self-importance. Leopold believed that he had no need to behave according to the law, or to conform to social conventions. His hedonism was what determined his actions. He, in fact, attacked the testimony of Doctor Krohn, the State's expert, by quoting from Krohn's textbook of psychiatry the section on paranoia, which fit Leopold very closely. Bachrach then turned to Loeb, and described him as schizophrenic, progressively withdrawing from reality into a delusional world where he was the master criminal. His personality was disintegrating, and he could not function on a day to day basis. His escalating criminal behavior was seen as the product of this underlying psychosis. As Darrow had done in his cross examination of the State's experts, Bachrach stressed that the State's experts had failed to find any evidence of mental illness because of the abbreviated, very surface examination in the office of the State's Attorney with many other people present. Under such circumstances, Bachrach maintained, a doctor would see only the surface and not understand the deeper motivating factors which would only be apparent in a more in depth private examination.

Clarence Darrow spoke next. He was reluctant to rely on the testimony of the defense experts, because, very simply and despite all of the understanding of Leopold and Loeb from their psychodynamics to their physical condition, it did not add up to the argument Darrow wanted to make. Because of their mental conditions, Leopold and Loeb were compelled to commit the murder. None of the expert testimony, singularly or in combination, was able to explain the crime. Therefore, Darrow chose to address the issue of mental disease and defect in the defendants in only the most general way. The crime could not be explained unless one assumed the defendants were mentally ill. Heredity and environment, not free will, determine behavior, according to Darrow. He made little reference to the scientific testimony; for instance, he stated, consistent with his philosophy of determinism, that the crime was somehow inherent in Loeb's organism that a remote ancestor sent down the seed that corrupted him. Darrow contended that there could be no individual blame because he was born with an emotional incapacity.

Darrow described Nathan Leopold, in a similar manner, as suffering from an emotional incapacity—a deficit of emotion along with an excess of intellect. He described Leopold as an intellectual machine running without any emotional balance. The crime, therefore, was due to imperfections in the machinery. Since the concept of responsibility does not apply to machines, individuals cannot be blamed for their conduct. He contended, therefore, that the defendants could not be responsible for the killing, but rather that society was to blame; that society had a need to punish people for things they had done, but that were essentially out of their control. The crime had no motive or purpose. It was senseless and random and, therefore, could only be explained on the basis of mental illness.

Darrow then went on in the rest of his argument to essentially put capital punishment on trial, rarely mentioning the defendants' issues of mental illness. He stated that hanging the defendants would accomplish nothing and would merely be for the purpose of vengeance. Darrow contended that capital punishment would not deter crime and that the violence inherent in it would only serve to lessen humankind's capacity for charity, love and understanding. Darrow concluded by saying, "If I can succeed, my greatest award and my greatest hope and my greatest compensation will be that I have done something for the tens of thousands of other boys, for the other unfortunates who must tread the same way that these poor youths have trod, that I have done something to help human understanding, to temper justice with mercy, to overcome hate with love". Hanging them would be a futile act of revenge—a gesture and an appeasement of the mob. It would accomplish nothing, not even deter crime as the State has contended; it would only be a savage act, one that would add its measure of violence to society and diminish man's capacity for understanding, love and charity.

Darrow also dealt with the rumors that there had been a million-dollar defense and he insisted that there was no such defense, and that payments for the defense psychiatrists were the same as those for the prosecution psychiatrists.

Recall that Darrow had previously complained that no minor had been sentenced to death on a plea of guilty in Illinois. He now said that never had a human being under 28 or 30 been so sentenced. "I have seen a court urged almost to the point of threats to hang two boys, in the face of science, in the face of philosophy, in the face of humanity, in the face of experience, in the face of all the better and more humane thought of the age." Darrow was in fact 80–90 years ahead of his time. It is striking that the United States Supreme Court, in recent years, in a series of cases, Roper v. Simmons (2005), Graham v. Florida, (2010), Miller v. Alabama, (2012) has indeed recognized the "science" which Darrow spoke of in 1924. The High Court received into evidence "amicus curiae" (friend of the court) briefs submitted by the American Psychological Association pointing out that the structure of an adolescent's brain is different from that of an adult, and that, therefore, an adolescent who has committed a crime cannot be judged to be blameworthy in the same sense as an adult who has a more fully developed brain.

Darrow went on to say, "So long as this terrible tool (that is, capital punishment) is to be used as a plaything without thought or consideration in seeking to inflame the mob with the thought that a boy must be hanged, or civilization will be hanged. We ought to get rid of it and get rid of it altogether for the protection of human life… I am aware that a court has more experience, more judgment and more kindliness than a jury. Then, Your Honor, it may hardly be fair to the court because I am aware that I have helped to place a serious burden upon your shoulders and at that, I have always meant to be your friend. But this was not an act of friendship. I know perfectly well that where responsibility is divided by twelve, it is easy to say, 'Away with him.' But Your Honor if these boys hang, you must do it. There can be no division of responsibility here. You must do it. You can never explain that the rest overpowered you. It must be your deliberate, cool, premeditated act without a chance to shift responsibility."

Darrow then stated that of the 90 people previously hanged in Chicago, only 3 had been hanged on a plea of guilty and only 1 in the last 30 years. "I have never yet tried a case where the State's Attorney did not say that it was the most cold-blooded, inexcusable, premeditated case that ever occurred. If it was murder, there never was such a murder. If it was robbery, there never was such a robbery. If it was a conspiracy, it was the most terrible conspiracy that ever happened… Poor little Bobby Franks suffered very little… It was all over in 15 minutes after he got into the car." Darrow said it was not cruel except that death is cruel. Darrow then spoke for two more hours, until the court was adjourned.

The next morning, Darrow continued his recital of the crime, the two boys wandering around the school in their attempts to select the victim and picking up Bobby Franks within site of their homes.

"The law can be vindicated without killing anyone else. It might shock the fine sensibilities of the State's counsel that this boy was put into a culvert and left after he was dead but, Your Honor… I can think, and only think, Your Honor of taking two boys, one eighteen and the other nineteen, irresponsible, weak, diseased, penning them in a cell, checking off the days, and the hours and minutes until they will be taken out and hanged… I can picture them, wakened in the gray light of morning, furnished a suit of clothes by the State, led to the scaffold, their feet tied, black caps drawn over their heads, stood on a trapdoor, the hangman pressing a spring so that it gives way under them. I can see them fall through space and stopped by the rope around the necks." Following this, Darrow continued to attack the death penalty by stating, "You can trace the burnings, the boilings, the drawings and quarterings, the hanging of people in England at the crossroads, carving them up and hanging them as examples for all to see. We can come down to the last century where nearly two hundred crimes were punishable by death… You can read the stories of the hangings on a high hill and the populace from miles around coming out to the scene that everybody might be awed into goodness. Hanging for picking pockets… Hangings for murder and men were murdered on the way there and on the way home. Hangings for poaching. Hanging for everything and hangings in public. Not shut up cruelly and brutally in a jail, out of the light of day…" Darrow asked what happened and then answered his own question, stating "Nothing."

Darrow, when court reconvened, started talking about the prosecution's experts. He talked about Loeb, stating, "I do not know what remote ancestor may have sent down the seed that corrupted him and I do not know through how many ancestors it may have passed until it reached Dickie Loeb… There is not an act in all this horrible tragedy that was not the act of a child, the act of a child wandering around in the morning of life."

Darrow then turned to Leopold's preoccupation with Nietzsche, stating, "The superman was a creation of Nietzsche, but it has permeated every college and university in the civilized world." He described Leopold as "a boy at sixteen or seventeen becoming obsessed with these doctrines. It was not a casual bit of philosophy for him, it was his life. He believed that he and Loeb were the supermen. There might have been others, but they were two. The ordinary commands of society were not for them." Darrow continued to note that many who read the philosophy of Nietzsche knew that it had no application in life, and that Leopold and Loeb's error was in believing it and Darrow stated that they could only have believed it because of their diseased minds.

Darrow also spoke about the cause of crime, "Crime has its cause. Perhaps all crimes do not have the same cause but they all have some cause. And people today are seeking to find out the cause. We lawyers never try to find out. Scientists are studying it. Criminologists are investigating it. But we lawyers go on and on, punishing, hanging and thinking that by general terror we can stamp out crime. It never occurs to the lawyer that crime has a cause, as certainly as disease and that the way to rationally treat any abnormal condition is to remove the cause."

> I do not know how much salvage there is in these two boys. I hate to say it in their presence but what is there to look forward to? I do not know but what Your Honor would be merciful if you tied a rope around their necks and let them die; merciful to them but not merciful to civilization and not merciful to those who would be left behind. I know that these boys are not fit to be at large. I believe they will not be until they pass through the next stage of life, at forty-five or fifty. Whether they will be then, I cannot tell. I'm not sure of this and I will not be there to help them.

As Darrow neared the conclusion of his address, he noted, "I have stood here for three months as one might stand at the ocean trying to sweep back the tide. I hope the seas are subsiding and the wind is falling and I believe they are but I wish to make no false pretense to the court."

> I know that the future is on my side. Your Honor stands between the past and the future. You may hang these boys but in doing so you will turn your face toward the past. You may save them and make it easier for every child that some time may stand where these boys stand.

Chapter 4
Judge Caverly's Sentencing

Judge Caverly indicated that, "[T]he State was in possession not only of the essential substantiating facts, but also of voluntary confessions on the part of the defendants. The plea of guilty, therefore, does not make a special case in favor of the defendants... The testimony introduced both by the prosecution and the defense has been detailed and elaborate, as though the case had been tried before a jury. It has been given the widest publicity and the public is so fully familiar with all its phases that it would serve no useful purpose to restate or analyze the evidence."

In addressing the physical, mental, and moral conditions of Leopold and Loeb, Judge Caverly stated, "They have been shown in essential respects to be abnormal. Had they been normal, they would not have committed the crime. It is beyond the province of this court as it is beyond the province of human science in its present state of development to predicate ultimate responsibility for human acts. At the same time, the court is willing to recognize that the careful analysis made of the life history of the defendants and of their present mental, emotional, and ethical condition has been of extreme interest and is a valuable contribution to criminology; and yet the court feels strongly that similar analysis made of other persons accused of a crime would reveal similar or different abnormalities. The value of such tests seems to lie in their applicability to crime and criminals in general. Since they concern the broad questions of human responsibility and legal punishment and are in no wise [sic] peculiar to these individual defendants, they may be deserving of legislative, but not of judicial consideration. For this reason, the court is satisfied that his judgment in the present case cannot be affected thereby. The testimony in this case reveals a crime of singular atrocity. It is, in a sense, inexplicable but it is not thereby rendered less inhuman or repulsive. It was deliberately planned and prepared for during a considerable period of time. It was executed with every feature of callousness and cruelty. And here the court will say, not for the purpose of extenuating guilt, but merely with the object of dispelling misapprehension that appears to have found lodgment in the public mind, that he is convinced by conclusive evidence that there was no abuse offered to the body of the victim. But it did not need that element to make the crime abhorrent to every instinct of humanity, and the court is satisfied

© Springer International Publishing AG 2018

D. L. Shapiro et al., *Retrying Leopold and Loeb*, SpringerBriefs in Psychology,

https://doi.org/10.1007/978-3-319-74600-5_4

that neither in the act itself, nor in its motive or lack of motive, nor in the antecedents of the offenders, can he find any mitigating circumstances."

Judge Caverly summarized the law and noted that people found guilty of murder could be punished by death or imprisoned for life or for a term not less than 14 years. Judge Caverly went on to state, "[T]he court is willing to meet his responsibilities. It would have been the path of least resistance to impose the extreme penalty of the law. In choosing imprisonment instead of death, the court is moved chiefly by the consideration of the age of the defendants, boys of eighteen and nineteen years. It is not for the court to say that he will not in any case enforce capital punishment as an alternative, but the court believes it is within his province to decline to impose the sentence of death on persons who are not of full age."

> This determination appears to be in accordance with the progress of criminal law all over the world and with the dictates of enlightened humanity. More than that, it seems to be in accordance with the precedents hitherto observed in this State. The records of Illinois show only two cases of minors who were put to death by legal process—to which number the court does not feel inclined to make an addition.

> Life imprisonment may not, at the moment, strike the public imagination as forcibly as would death by hanging; but to the offenders, particularly of the type they are, the prolonged suffering of years of confinement may well be the more severe form of retribution and expiation.

> The court feels it is proper to add a final word concerning the effect of the parole law upon the punishment upon these defendants. In the case of such atrocious crimes, it is entirely within the discretion of the Department of Public Welfare never to admit these defendants to parole. To such a policy, the court urges them strictly to adhere. If this course is preserved in, the punishment of these defendants it will both satisfy the ends of justice and safeguard the interests of society.

The judge then announced his sentence. For the crime of murder, confinement in the penitentiary at Joliet for the term of their natural lives and, for the crime of kidnapping for ransom, similar confinement for the term of 99 years was imposed.

Chapter 5
A Re-examination

As we noted earlier, in the 1920s, we were really in an era when psychiatry was in its infancy, was just coming out of the consulting room, and stepping into the courtroom. There really was only one approach to the treatment of mental disorders—psychoanalysis (treatments such as cognitive behavioral therapy, behavior modification, systematic desensitization, did not make their appearance until the 1960s or later). While the ideas about unconscious motives directing human behavior were intriguing to many, the idea that someone could commit a crime, especially a violent one, was difficult for people to accept. Consider State's Attorney Crowe's closing argument in which he stressed the months of planning and premeditation that went into the crime; anything that was that involved clearly did not have the mark of mental illness.

However, a whole other area of inquiry now exists that did not in the 1920s. Even though there was some evidence of brain abnormalities in Nathan Leopold's skull x rays, no one could quite understand the significance of these findings, nor their relationship to Leopold's peculiar belief system. While Loeb was described by some of the doctors as psychopathic, at that time in history, there was no body of knowledge that related abnormalities in brain structure and function to psychopathy. This connection was not well developed until Robert Hare's work in the late 1980s and early 1990s (Hare, 1991).

What we are proposing here is a retrospective look at the observations made of Leopold and Loeb in 1924 and, if their trial were occurring today, what might the expert testimony be? While their mental illnesses were described differently by different doctors, one of the consistent themes was Nathan Leopold's "superman belief" and how it exempted him from the laws of society, which was actually delusional in its extent. Similarly, psychopathy, as displayed by Loeb, has a variety of neurodevelopmental abnormalities that have been well documented in the literature. As noted earlier, neither Leopold nor Loeb would have, in all likelihood, committed the crime by themselves. This is why we are calling it a "perfect storm" born from an interface between two very distinct kinds of psychopathology that resulted in a horrific and baffling crime.

© Springer International Publishing AG 2018
D. L. Shapiro et al., *Retrying Leopold and Loeb*, SpringerBriefs in Psychology,
https://doi.org/10.1007/978-3-319-74600-5_5

5.1   Nathan Leopold

As noted earlier, the way Nathan Leopold used the Nietzschean notion of the "uebermensch" or "superman" was so far removed from the original concept in Nietzsche's *Thus Spoke Zarathustra* that the distortions were clearly delusional. Recall that the Nietzschean idea was of a creative mind who, despite all opposition, would proliferate ideas that would lead to the betterment of mankind (Nietzsche & Kaufmann, 1995). It was not the hedonistic, self-serving idea that Nathan Leopold endorsed. Neither was Leopold's idea of disdaining all emotion as weakness, believing that he was an example of pure intellect, found in Nietzsche's writings. If anything, it was quite the opposite. Nietzsche believed in the importance of emotions. Nietzsche was especially critical of religion because he felt that religion sought to stifle natural expressions of feelings. (Perhaps his atheism was the one area in which Leopold's belief was consistent with that of Nietzsche). Finally, Leopold's notion that being a "superman" put him above society's rules and regulations and that he could violate the law, even by committing murder, is found nowhere in Nietzsche's work. It was clearly a mental illness that led to the distortions made by Leopold when trying to justify his behavior as that of a "superman."

What do we know about the neurological basis of delusional thinking, especially in the case of what appears to be a delusional system without the accompanying thought disorder seen in schizophrenia? Unfortunately, very little, since virtually all neurological studies dealing with the etiology of delusions puts them within the framework of paranoid schizophrenia. There are few studies that deal with paranoid thinking distinct from a schizophrenic disorder. Therefore, we cannot know for sure whether the neurological constructs being described are really relevant to the paranoia or to the schizophrenia. Nevertheless, some of the ideas seem to describe quite precisely the nature of delusional thinking.

For instance, Corlett, Taylor, Wang, Fletcher, and Krystal (2010) describe delusions as resulting from abnormalities in the circuitry of the brain, which prevent the individual from adequately responding to "prediction errors." Put simply, if a person is delusional, he or she "screens out" stimuli which would challenge their misperceptions of reality and only accept those that confirm the belief. These researchers believe that frontostriatal circuits, along with the amygdala and parietal cortex are involved. Since information is represented in the brain through the formation and strengthening of synaptic connections between neurons, abnormalities in the neurotransmitters are the basis of delusions, in that there is a failure to properly encode the precision of prediction and prediction errors. More specifically, there is an excessive and inappropriate dopamine signaling which makes coincidental events perceived as "highly salient." In other words, disparate events that would normally be perceived as separate or at best coincidental, take on a specific meaning of importance to the delusional individual. Delusional patients lack the ability to use learned information to challenge their experience. These researchers describe this as an "aberration of sensory and affective perception." Sophisticated neuroimaging techniques, such as functional MRI's, PET scans, and SPECT scans, can look at these abnormalities in the circuitry.

Other researchers, such as Puente and Tonkonogy (2009) also note that delusions of grandeur are often seen in individuals with lesions of the frontal lobe and fronto-temporal areas. They also note the involvement of the limbic system, consistent with the references to the amygdala in the previously noted research.

Morimoto et al. (2002) noted that delusional disorder includes a "dopamine psychosis" and that different presentations of the disorder may be due to etiological heterogeneity of the disorder. These researchers speak of a possible genetic component and address what they call the dysfunctional cognitive processes. In short, ideas upon which these individuals tend to make inferences are typically based on less information than that utilized by most people. Conclusions are drawn without stopping to consider alternative explanations for a particular phenomenon. This inability to consider alternatives is seen as due to an imbalance in the neurotransmitters.

Kunert, Norra, and Hoff (2007) noted a wide variety of conditions that may give rise to delusional thinking including brain tumors, traumatic brain injuries, Huntington's Chorea, endocrine abnormalities (especially hypothyroidism), impaired renal function, and neurotoxic agents. They further note that patients with delusional syndromes (especially those related to limbic disorder) have unusual emotional experiences which are the building blocks of the delusions. Injuries to the subcortical areas, such as the basal ganglia, can result in specific dysfunction of the neurotransmitter systems, which, through cognitive and emotional changes, become delusions. These researchers also point to the fact that there is a significant correlation between the extent of a delusional disorder and regional cerebral blood flow in the left frontal and frontal medial regions. They also note that, while schizophrenics who have delusions often show clear neuropsychological dysfunction, these impairments are rarely seen in delusional disorders. Basically, elaborate delusions require intact neurocognitive functioning. Acute delusions are often connected to dopaminergic or noradrenergic hyperactivity. They observe that this hyperactivity can be seen as consistent with the jumping to conclusions and the unwillingness to admit anything that would refute the delusional beliefs, as well as the absence of any cognitive impairment. In summary, many of the studies reviewed by these researchers demonstrate dysfunctions of the prefrontal, limbic and subcortical regions.

In a very extensive review, Bell and Halligan (2013) noted that while there have been several hypotheses about the neurodevelopmental basis for delusional thinking, as yet, there does not exist an integrated review of the neuropsychological and neurological models of delusions. They summarize a number of studies which unfortunately do not seem to reach similar conclusions, although it could always be argued that delusional ideas can be different from one another and consequently have different etiologies. One of the most well known, the Capgras delusion (believing that family and friends are really impostors masquerading as these close individuals), seem to be based on right hemisphere dysfunction. There is hemispheric asymmetry, as the right hemisphere reveals greater activation in imaging studies than the left. The right hemisphere is seen as being associated with "coarser" associations, while the left with more focused associations. The right hemisphere then may demonstrate loose and uncommon associations which may result in creativity or, in its more extreme forms, delusional thinking. On the other hand, the researchers noted that functional imaging literature demonstrates increased activation of the left frontal and left temporal areas and persecutory delusions in particular demonstrate activation on both sides of the brain. The right hemisphere is described by these authors as a "discrepancy detector" and, if damaged, will result in the individual being unable to reject an abnormal belief or hypothesis, consequently solidifying a delusional system. They suggest that some of the discrepancies in the findings might possibly be explained by the fact that the increased activation may not represent the etiology of the delusion, but rather an attempt at compensation or adaptation. It becomes an example of the old question, "which came first, the chicken or the egg?" Other studies have demonstrated ventricular enlargement, temporal lobe volume reduction (especially in the medial temporal lobe areas and the superior temporal gyrus) and structural abnormalities in the corpus callosum and in the prefrontal cortex. Imaging studies have also demonstrated contradictory findings. Some functional imaging studies have illustrated problems in the areas described above, but also in the parahippocampal areas. Some SPECT scan studies have also demonstrated decreased activation in the left frontal and medial temporal areas. A rather consistent finding across several studies is that patients with delusions and hallucinations demonstrate excessive pruning of synaptic connections in the prefrontal cortex. Strozier (2004) demonstrated some of this "pruning" in victims of sexual abuse. Mutluer et al. (2017) noted that Posttraumatic Stress Disorder occurring as a result of childhood sexual abuse has been shown to be related to a smaller amygdala, hippocampus, anterior cingulate, and a thinner prefrontal cortex. EEG abnormalities have been noted in 54% of children with abuse histories, while similar abnormalities are found in only 27% of a sample of children who had not been abused. The more severe the abuse, the greater the impact on brain function. Still other studies reveal that focal injuries in the limbic system can result in delusions, as can left temporal lesions. One other fact that appears consistent across studies is that intact cognitive functioning (distinct from the thinking deterioration seen in schizophrenia) seems to be essential for the development of elaborate delusional processes. It has also been observed that the left cerebral cortex may be underdeveloped and the left hippocampus smaller in abuse victims. Abuse can also damage the amygdala. Repeated abuse results in the amygdala signaling danger even when there is no real threat (what is described in the DSM-5 as hyperarousal). Abuse has also been found to decrease serotonin levels leading to depression and impulsive aggression.

One of the other illnesses that can be associated with delusional thinking is, of course, dementia. We generally associate dementia with people who are older, but some recent research (Baker et al., 2015) revealed evidence of dementia in younger people as well. Surprisingly, they found that toxic amyloid buildup in the brain appeared to be present irrelevant of age or health. In fact, some seniors in the study did not have any greater amount of amyloid buildup than that seen in the brains of young adults. The estimated prevalence rate of early onset Alzheimer's and related dementias is 4–5% of the 4.5 million individuals with dementia in the United States (Alzheimer's Association, n.d.). At the same time, however, the progressive cognitive decline and neurological symptoms typical of early onset dementia were not seen in Leopold and the delusional beliefs are generally not associated with early onset dementia.

Calcification in the brain is another area that might need to be examined; recall that Leopold had osteosclerosis and an obliteration of some of the suture lines in the brain. This calcium buildup is often found in the basal ganglia, although other parts of the brain may be affected as well. Of course, the basal ganglia is found deep within the brain and evidence of it would only be found using sophisticated neuro-imaging techniques not available in 1924 (only a skull x-ray was available at that time).

There is a need for future research into the neuropsychological correlates of Delusional Disorder. It is still one of the most under-researched disorders. There is a low prevalence of the disorder, primarily due to the high level of functioning and lack of insight of delusional patients.

Because of all the historical confusion regarding terms and definitions, the literature has generally been unhelpful in separating Delusional Disorder from other disorders, including Paranoid Schizophrenia, Cyclic Psychosis, Brief Reactive Psychosis, and Delusional Misidentification Syndromes.

In addition, little empirical research has been done to clarify the neuropsychological mechanisms underlying delusions, especially in patients with Delusional Disorder. The comparisons that have been made are those of patients with Paranoia, as opposed to Non-paranoia, Schizophrenia, rather than those with a diagnosed Delusional Disorder. Previous reviews have been based on persecutory delusions and this is by far the most prevalent among delusional types (Nathan Leopold had a grandiose delusion).

Delusional Disorder is characterized by false beliefs held with firm conviction despite evidence to the contrary typically accompanied by strong affect and exaggerated vigilance. By definition, functioning is not markedly impaired and behavior is not odd or bizarre. The *Diagnostic and Statistical Manual, Fifth Edition* (DSM-5), describes a delusion as "a false belief based on incorrect inference about external reality that is firmly sustained despite what almost everyone else believes and despite what constitutes incontrovertible and obvious proof or evidence to the contrary. The belief is not one ordinarily accepted by other members of the person's culture or subculture." Delusions may also occur in non-psychotic mental disorders, such as Unipolar Depression, Bipolar Disorder, and Posttraumatic Stress Disorder. Delusions can also be found in association with some neurophysiological conditions, such as dementia, temporal lobe epilepsy, Huntington's disease, Parkinson's disease, multiple sclerosis, and traumatic brain injury (American Psychiatric Association, 2013).

It has also been noted that most studies agree that Delusional Disorder is predominantly an illness of middle-to-late adult life (Nathan Leopold, of course, was 19 years old, but recall that his skull x-rays revealed an abnormality, a premature calcification, that the doctors said usually occurs in individuals 30–35 years old, not 19).

Correlations between brain disorders and delusional symptoms may suggest that impaired brain function is likely to play a role in the pathogenesis of Delusional Disorder. Research shows that Delusional Disorder can arise from different injuries or dysfunctions of various brain systems. Lesions in the limbic system and subcortical structures, primarily left-sided, have been traditionally associated with delusions but not all patients with injuries in these regions develop delusions, suggesting that there are further predisposing factors. In addition, there have been some associations found between right hemisphere impairment and delusional beliefs. Right hemisphere damage may involve impairment of the belief evaluation system that is located in the right cerebral hemisphere. It is suggested that the region associated with this is located in the right frontal lobe. Therefore, it is predicted that patients with these types of delusions (brain injury related delusions) will have right frontal damage. However, there is no evidence yet for a clear functional asymmetry in Delusional Disorder.

An area of controversy has to do with whether or not areas of the brain that deal with cognition are intact and this appears to be somewhat inconsistent. Neuropsychological impairment in Delusional Disorder is often seen as minor because otherwise complex delusions could not be developed. Therefore, neuropsychological assessment may well focus on subtle brain dysfunction.

Some authors have also argued that the cause of delusional, specifically paranoid symptoms, refer to a hyperdopaminergic state in the brain. It has been proposed that these patients have a hyperreactive dopamine system.

Researchers hypothesized that different kinds of unusual experiences are the basis for different kinds of delusions. This initial factor is what prompts the delusional belief and, together with cognitive biases, such as attributional and data-gathering biases, are responsible for the content in the delusion. The central point is that delusional patients have a failure in their ability to discard a belief that is implausible and inconsistent with their previous knowledge. This failure prevents the person from rejecting the belief, even in the light of very strong countervailing evidence. This is believed to arise from a reasoning deficit associated with the right frontal cortex. However, these impairments have been found in delusions resulting from brain damage or pathology and have not yet been confirmed in delusional patients who do not have such brain impairment. Delusional individuals overreact to threatening stimuli. Individuals with persecutory delusions have a misperception of threat in ambiguous or inappropriate situations. Jumping to conclusions seems to be a part of that. In short, there seems to be a contradiction that there is an initial automatic preattentional bias toward threatening material but a subsequently controlled attentional bias away from the threat. This is sometimes described as a pattern of vigilance-avoidance (two of the criteria for PTSD) (American Psychiatric Association, 2013). It has also been proposed that self referent information must be particularly important for deluded patients. The delusional individuals selectively pay attention to threatening information and, therefore, have a better recall of this type of data, which could explain the maintenance of delusions and resistance to change. They selectively attend to the information that confirms their delusional belief and tend to ignore information contrary to their beliefs. This has been referred to as a bias against disconfirmatory evidence. Notably, this bias against disconfirmatory evidence seems to be independent of other cognitive measures, such as memory, intelligence and executive functions (recall that Nathan Leopold's scores on the intelligence test were extremely high).

In summary, deluded patients seem to show strong attentional biases, including exaggerated perception of threat even in non-threatening situations, and a preference for self-referent information. Avoidance of threatening stimuli, which may be used to reduce anxiety and maintain the delusional system, better recall of threatening or self referent information and avoidance of information that is inconsistent with their beliefs, all explain the persistence of the delusional belief. It has also been suggested that anxiety and depression are often found in delusional individuals and this would make sense in that the delusions are constructed to maintain self-esteem and to avoid anxiety.

The subtle cognitive deficits are only detectable by the use of neuropsychological assessment. Individuals with delusions request fewer pieces of information before making a decision compared with clinical controls. This most likely leads to the rapid acceptance of beliefs, even if there is limited evidence to support them. Biases in data gathering will enable the rapid acceptance of implausible explanations. A tendency toward an early acceptance of hypotheses may contribute to the formation of delusions. From an evolutionary point of view, delusions develop to counteract a severe social failure. In particular, grandiose delusions would work by increasing the social value of the individual, therefore increasing the chance to gain friends, allies and other social benefits. (In Leopold's case, he did not seem to be interested in gaining friends, but the social benefit that he would gain by virtue of being a superman was that he was not bound by any rules of society and could indulge in his hedonistic philosophy—namely, that he could do whatever he wanted if it gave him pleasure.) Most research, unfortunately, deals with persecutory delusions, and there is a question as to how much it would generalize to grandiose delusions. Most cognitive neuropsychiatric research has shown that at least some delusional thinking is neuropsychological in origin. However, there is limited research on this. Fujii, Ahmed, and Takeshita (1999) studied patients with erotomanic Delusional Disorder using the Wisconsin Card Sorting Test and found that these patients showed deficits in cognitive flexibility and associative learning. The results suggested an executive functioning deficit. Erotomania (and possibly grandiosity) might be associated with deficits in cognitive flexibility and associative learning mediated by frontal subcortical systems. According to the authors, these patients with Delusional Disorder may have a cognitive set that predisposes them to make conclusions with significantly less evidence than normal subjects.

In summary, there seems to be a bit of controversy since impairment in areas such as limbic and subcortical structures on the left side is highlighted in some research and in the right frontal lobe in other research. A consistent factor seems to be that there is damage to the belief evaluation system associated with the right frontal cortex.

However, this jumping-to-conclusion bias could rely on an impulsivity or motivational factor that has not been thus far investigated. Individuals with Delusional Disorder may be poor at representing the mental states of other people. Delusions seem to be directly related to impaired executive functioning.

In summary, delusional individuals show a bias toward paying attention to certain kinds of information, particularly with regard to threats, self-reference and delusional confirmatory information. Deluded individuals are biased toward the search for an explanation and they show a very strong need for closure, thus the jumping to conclusions. They feel a strong need for an explanation of a strange experience and take the first one available. That belief evaluation system which seems to be located in the right frontal lobe should help the individual reject the misbelief. In delusional patients without a history of brain damage, the process might be slightly biased, leading to the acceptance of the ungrounded or implausible beliefs. Maintenance of delusional beliefs could come from the reduction in anxiety this provided by the fact of having an explanation.

If we had had this level of understanding of the workings of the brain in 1924, how might the assessment and testimony regarding Nathan Leopold be different? The abnormalities discovered by skull x-rays in Leopold's case would have been further studied with the use of sophisticated brain imaging, such as a PET scan which can observe the metabolic activity in the brain, a phenomenon which a static skull x-ray could not reveal. The hypopituitarism that was noted in the examination of Nathan Leopold could also have been correlated with impaired brain development. There were also several symptoms suggesting a genetic disorder, including the premonitory signs of kidney disease (well documented in the family history) and a possible etiologic factor in the formation of delusional thinking. His lack of resistance to disease, high fevers, Bright's disease, prominence of the eyes and facial asymmetry, as well as the dermographia, involuted thymus gland, history of gastrointestinal distress, frontal and occipital headaches, and neurocirculatory asthenia, could, these days, be studied through extensive genetic testing.

We have reviewed the possible neurological correlates to his delusional thinking that coexist with his total hedonism, lack of affect, emotional detachment, as well as his superior cognitive abilities; all suggest the possibility of frontal lobe dysfunction which could, of course, be studied with the imaging techniques noted above.

As far as the expert testimony, there would, of course, be more emphasis on the fact that what is perceived as a psychological disorder by some and as cold-blooded evil by others is all related to the human brain. Not only is the brain functioning causally related to behavior, but various disorders caused by abuse and trauma have neurological sequelae (recall the sexual abuse by his governess). This testimony would also be more easily received by juries as lay people are always more impressed by some physical or structural disorder than by "merely" psychological problems. If this trial were being held today, the experts would stress the interaction between the psychological and neurological and not see them as separate phenomena.

5.2   Richard Loeb

As noted earlier, Richard Loeb was described by the experts at the time of the trial as quite immature, having emotional reactions to situations consistent with those of a 5 or 6-year-old. His judgment was equally child-like and there was an extreme dichotomy or pathological discord between emotions and judgment on the one hand and intellect on the other. An emotional detachment allowed Loeb to discuss the murder with no emotion or feeling and no remorse or grief. It was in fact an affective incapacity. Loeb was described as incapable of taking in the emotional meaning of a situation. However, he did want to read about it in the newspapers. He was capable of taking in facts and could communicate them well, but he had no capacity for empathy and was not even aware of his own emotions. At trial, Loeb's behavior was very inappropriate, as he would laugh and joke about different aspects of the crime. There was a curious confluence of two very disturbed personalities—Loeb, who was incapable of the appropriate affect and Leopold, who felt no affect because he delusionally believed himself to be the "uebermensch" who could approach everything in the world as an intellectual exercise. While Clarence Darrow could not understand the reasons behind these oddities, he was a skilled enough attorney to know that in front of a liberal judge, there would be a chance of demonstrating that these affective incapacities were consistent with a serious mental disorder and that in front of a jury, it would have been disastrous. A jury would merely believe that the lack of affect was proof of Leopold and Loeb being depraved, cold-blooded killers who deserved to be hanged. Again, the discrepancy between affect and intellect could be correlated with disruption of the functioning of the frontal lobes, with intellect and cognition intact, but an inability to appreciate how other people feel. The skull x-rays used in 1924 could not reveal these peculiarities in functioning, while sophisticated brain imaging techniques available now can.

Many of these traits displayed by Loeb are consistent, as noted earlier, with what is now described as psychopathy. Loeb demonstrated superficiality, having no deep interests and an inability to complete projects he had undertaken. He was glib in his conversations and had a "gift for gab." He was very skillful, to a pathological degree, in lying. This appeared to derive from his skill in playing his mother and his governess against one another, lying to both and not being caught in the lies. (Imaging studies have revealed increased activation in the prefrontal and parietal cortex during lying.) Similarly, his ability to con and manipulate appeared to have some of its origins in these interactions. He also demonstrated the ability to "use" others in his relationships with his friends. His lack of guilt and remorse was obviously demonstrated in his responses to the crime, along with feelings of superiority. He felt that he was the most intelligent master criminal. The lack of concern for his own safety manifested itself in fearlessness, reckless driving, being involved in car chases, jumping out of a moving car and going out on Lake Michigan in a small boat during a storm. He also demonstrated what the literature on psychopathy describes as "criminal versatility" being involved in a variety of criminal activities. He began stealing at the age of 8. He would steal cars, commit arson, and turn in false fire alarms again for the thrill. He would later discuss the elements of the crimes with friends and the police, "knowing something they did not". As noted earlier, he did sustain a head injury at age 15, which could possibly be related to the lack of emotion (although his criminal activity clearly predated this head injury).

It has been observed that when psychopaths imagine others experiencing pain, the brain regions that are associated with empathy and concern for others fail to activate or connect with the brain areas involved in emotional processing and decision making. Some studies have even demonstrated activation in the areas of the brain having to do with pleasurable feelings, when the psychopath imagines inflicting pain on another. Many of these studies regarding disrupted affective functioning seem to relate to dysfunction in the amygdala (Decety & Moriguchi, 2007).

Raine (1993, 2014) notes that the prefrontal cortex plays a critical part in the regulation and control of emotions and behavior. He also observes that the angular gyrus, an area at the intersection of the parietal, temporal, and occipital lobes connects and integrates information from several modalities in order to perform complex functions. In Raine's studies, of people who have been convicted of murder, it was found that there was a significantly lower glucose metabolism than controls. The angular gyrus is involved with this metabolism. He also reviews the investigations of abnormalities in the functioning of the amygdala and hippocampus in violent offenders. Functional disturbance in the hippocampus, according to some studies cited by Raine, also demonstrate higher scores on psychopathy on the Psychopathy Check List Revised (Hare, 1991). Disruptions of hippocampal functioning can result in socially inappropriate behaviors, as well as the tendency to have difficulties recognizing and appraising stimuli in social situations. Fear conditioning and emotional responsivity, both associated, as noted before, with the amygdala, seem to lead to not only rage attacks, but predatory violent behavior as well. The posterior cingulate has also been demonstrated to function poorly in adult criminal psychopaths. There appears to be an inability to think back and understand how their personal behaviors can affect and harm others.

There is always a tendency to try to simplify the contributions of a particular psychological or neurological dysfunction to behavior. In fact, it is a very complex interaction among many impaired neural systems.

In adult psychopaths, there appear to be misfirings in the prefrontal and limbic systems, poorer functioning in the angular gyrus, and abnormalities in the posterior cingulate, amygdala, and hippocampus. The reduced activity in the amygdala of psychopaths has its behavioral correlates in the phenomenon of the psychopath just not thinking about or even considering the fact that they manipulate and con other people. Since there is impaired firing in the amygdala, there is nothing to constrain the behavior or to result in feelings of guilt and remorse. Some of these individuals describe emotions as "dead" and the need to go to extreme lengths to experience emotions (such as killing for the thrill of it?).

As noted earlier, when discussing Loeb's physical examination, he had a very low resting heart rate. High resting heart rates are found in anxiety, depression, and schizophrenia. Only antisocial and aggressive behavior seems to be linked to low heart rate. This same phenomenon is linked to fearlessness and lack of empathy.

Low arousal is an unpleasant emotional state and such people will generally seek out stimulation such as interaction with other people to increase arousal levels. Psychopaths have very low arousal levels, so they experience intense tension restlessness. They need to seek a victim to experience excitement in the antisocial activity and, following the activity experience, a sense of relief from tension. This underarousal in psychopaths comes from the poor fear conditioning and leads to a poorly developed conscience. Structural brain deficits in the left frontal cortex along with a variety of psychological risk factors and deficits in the amygdala and hippocampus are often observed in neuroimaging studies of people convicted of murder. The connections between the prefrontal areas (involved in coding social and emotional stimuli) and the limbic system are crucial, as they relate to appropriate emotional responses within a social setting. If the connections are damaged, we see emotional blunting and a lack of empathy. The lack of autonomic emotional responsivity results in an inability to reason effectively in a variety of situations, especially those that are risky. There are many observations regarding the specific parts of the frontal lobes involved in violent behavior, but they are far more complex than we can cover in this volume. Suffice it to say that deficits in the prefrontal cortex and its connections to the limbic system can lead to problems with fear conditioning, inhibition of behavioral responses, moral judgment capabilities, and the ability to defer gratification. As noted earlier, psychopaths not only lack the ability to feel empathy when someone else is in pain but cannot even look into themselves to understand their own motivations, thoughts, and feelings. This leads to a lack of sensitivity to emotional states, their own as well as those of others.

More specifically, the amygdala, which is involved in regulation of emotions, has been found to be structurally abnormal in psychopaths. Manifestations are lack of affect, lack of emotional depth, and deficiencies in fear responses. Raine observes that there are 13 nuclei in the amygdala, and 3 of the 13 are deformed in psychopaths. These three deal with fear conditioning, attentional strength and avoidance learning (i.e., learning to do things that avoid punishment). This is one of the reasons that we see high recidivism rates or, in common parlance, the inability to learn from experience. Raine further states that these deficits most likely are genetic and not caused by traumatic brain injury.

In a similar manner, there are deficits in the hippocampal areas, with the right hippocampus being larger than the left. This is sometimes called structural asymmetry. The hippocampus, like the amygdala, seems to play a role in autonomic response and fear conditioning. Raine cites the work of Boccardi et al. (2010) who note the abnormal hippocampal shape in offenders with psychopathy. The hippocampus, according to these researchers, helps an individual to remember a particular place and associate it with a particular punishment. It also helps in the regulating of emotions through projections to the parts of the brain that modulate both defensive and reactive aggression and predatory attacks. The role of the corpus callosum's 200 million nerve fibers that connect different brain regions, remains somewhat controversial. Some studies suggest that, in psychopaths, there are excessive connections, while others demonstrate decreased connectivity. Again, like the amygdala, it is believed that these connective abnormalities are not due to a disease process or to trauma, but rather represent a genetic process. Other researchers have pointed to the role of the striatum in social behavior and disturbances in the striatum in psychopathy. The striatum is the module input to the basal ganglia. Total Psychopathy Checklist Revised scores and Factor 2 scores (the impulsive antisocial factor) were associated with larger striatal subnuclei volumes and increased volume in focal areas throughout the striatum. Abnormal functional connectivity with other areas of the brain, notably the dorsolateral prefrontal cortex, was already noted.

Finally, from the point of view of describing and measuring psychopathy, one of the most well known and extensively researched instruments is Hare's Psychopathy Check List Revised (PCL-R). This instrument has two factors. The first is interpersonal style and the second is behavioral. The examiner rates the subject as 0 (not present), 1 (partially or maybe present) or 2 (definitely present). The rating is usually done by both an interview and a review of collateral sources. Here, of course, we must depend on history and behavioral descriptions, since Loeb is not around for us to interview. Relying on his history, we see scores of "2" that is definitely present on glibness, superficial charm (so described by peers, police and attorneys), grandiose sense of self-worth (most brilliant criminal in Chicago), pathological lying, cunning, and manipulative (peer relationships, as well as relationships with governess and mother), lack of remorse and guilt, shallow affect, callousness, lack of empathy (no emotional reaction to offense), and failure to accept responsibility for his own actions (saying that Leopold was the one who struck the child with the chisel). These are the components of Factor 1, the interpersonal style variables. On Factor 2, the behavioral, he receives a score of "2" on need for stimulation and proneness to boredom, impulsivity, irresponsibility and juvenile delinquency (breaking windows, jumping out of moving cars and previous criminal behavior). He also receives scores of "1" (possibly present) on parasitic lifestyle, poor behavioral controls, early behavioral problems and lack of realistic long-term goals (he will serve a few years in prison, come out, and lead a productive life). One other dimension which appears on the Check List, promiscuous sexual behavior, does not load on either Factor 1 or 2, but is listed because it is frequently seen in psychopaths (note that Loeb's first sexual encounter led to a sexually-transmitted disease). Criminal versatility, which we have also seen in his many petty crimes, does not load on either Factor. When we add together the scores on Factors 1 and 2, we obtain a score of 28, which is very close to the cutoff score of 30 suggested by Hare for psychopathy. Other studies have suggested a lower cutoff score of 26, in which case Loeb would clearly fit within the range designated as psychopathy (Hare, 1991).

In summary, we have in the interaction of Nathan Leopold and Richard Loeb a perfect storm; an interaction of personality and psychopathology that led to a brutal crime. Neither would have committed the crime on their own, but the synergy was deadly. Leopold had a delusional belief about being a superman and convinced Loeb that he too belonged to this class of individuals. Loeb was a psychopath who, because of abnormal brain structure and circuitry, was incapable of having normal fear conditioning, anticipating the consequences of his behavior and learning from experience. Both believed that they could commit "the perfect crime," Loeb because of his belief that he was the most brilliant criminal in Chicago and Leopold because of a delusion that he was a "superman" and was not bound by the ordinary laws that govern society. This created a unique and unusual confluence of two disordered personalities that led to a brutal and senseless homicide of a 14-year-old boy that was called the "Crime of the Century" in 1924.

Chapter 6
Re-Imagining the Closing Argument

Clarence Darrow was a towering figure in the world of law, defending the indefensible, fighting to save many people from execution because of the sheer weight of his convictions and the eloquent way in which he expressed them. Recall that in this case, Darrow decided that strategically he could not utilize the expert testimony as the basis for his final argument. While the experts were distinguished psychiatrists, none were able to reach a causal nexus between the mental disorders and the crime, such that they could testify that because of mental disease or defect, Leopold and Loeb could not appreciate the wrongfulness of their behavior (the criteria for an insanity defense). The very extensive planning, the demands for ransom and the attempts to cover their tracks, all spoke to a complete understanding of the wrongfulness of their behavior. It was for this reason that Darrow chose not to pursue an insanity defense and entered guilty pleas on their behalf, thereby attempting to use the expert testimony as mitigation. Darrow had a shot at this, since Judge John Caverly had a reputation as a serious, scholarly individual who was liberal in his judicial philosophy. However, once again, if he used the expert testimony, he would still have to demonstrate how the mental disorders resulted in a compulsion to commit the crime or, at the very least, demonstrate how the factors in Leopold and Loeb's backgrounds led to the specific crime. Darrow was unable to see the connection and was afraid that Judge Caverly would not either. (In fact, Darrow was correct in that Caverly made only passing reference to the mental condition of the defendants and chose to sentence them to life imprisonment rather than to death.) However, what would have happened if Darrow knew about the neurological basis of delusional disorder and psychopathy that we now know? Recall that Darrow, being a determinist and not believing in free will, had actually set the stage for this very type of testimony. He said of Loeb, "One of two things happened to this boy; that this terrible crime was inherent in his organism, and came from some ancestor, or it came through his education and training after he was born... I do not know what remote ancestors may have sent down the seed that corrupted him, and I do not know through how many ancestors it may have passed until it reached Dickie Loeb. All I know is, it is true, and there is not a biologist in the world who will say I am

© Springer International Publishing AG 2018

D. L. Shapiro et al., *Retrying Leopold and Loeb*, SpringerBriefs in Psychology,

https://doi.org/10.1007/978-3-319-74600-5_6

not right… Is Dickey Loeb to blame because out of the infinite forces that conspired to form him, the forces that were at work producing him ages before he was born, because out of these infinite combinations he was born without [emotional capacity]? … Is he to blame for what he did not have and never had? Is he to blame that his machine is imperfect?"

Regarding Leopold, Darrow said, Nathan "was just a half boy, an intellect, an intellectual machine going without balance and without a governor, seeking to find out everything there was to life intellectually; seeking to solve every philosophy, but using his intellect only." According to Darrow, Nathan was also blameless, suffering from emotional incapacity. He had an excess of intellect and a deficit of emotion. This led to the central part of Darrow's argument, that crime was a consequence of imperfections in the machine. The concept of responsibility was not applicable to the machine and, for that reason, individuals were not to blame for their actions; neither Leopold nor Loeb were responsible for the killing of Bobby Franks. The remainder of his eloquent closing argument essentially put the death penalty on trial.

With our current knowledge, however, we can well imagine Darrow saying something like the following, before he gets to his indictment of capital punishment:

> We are faced with an inexplicable crime of violence, which on its surface seems vicious, cold-blooded and premeditated. However, if we look beneath the surface, which the doctors hired by the State did not do, we see quite a different set of circumstances. We have two brilliant, privileged young men who enter into an agreement to kill someone for the thrill of it and to prove that they could commit the perfect crime and escape detection. But what could we learn if we go beyond the surface? We will find that young Mr. Leopold was delusional, a condition which the psychiatrists and psychologists describe as an intact false belief that is resistant to challenge from external sources of information. Leopold read deeply the works of the German philosopher Nietzsche, who spoke in his works of the "uebermensch" or superman who was above the beliefs of society because he had a gift for seeing what the true realities were and was placed on earth to teach these truths to society over the course of many years for the betterment of society. Nathan Leopold, because of his own psychological deficits misinterpreted this compassionate philosophy and turned it into a delusional belief that he himself was a superman and for that reason was above the morals of society—that he could even commit murder because it was akin to pinning a butterfly on a paper to be observed and involved the same degree of decision making as deciding whether or not to have pie with dinner. But where do such delusions come from? For many years, we did not know. Now, the science of neurology has demonstrated that such delusional thinking comes from lesions of the frontal lobe and impaired connections between these frontal lobes and structures of the limbic system such as the basal ganglia. The impairment in these connections renders an individual who is delusional incapable of self-correcting feedback. Such an individual does not have the capacity to challenge his own distorted beliefs. His brain and its infinite connections make it impossible to do so. All messages in the human brain are transmitted from one part of the brain to another by neurotransmitters, chemicals that move the information from one place to another. Brain imaging studies, as explained by our doctors clearly point to the deficits in these neurotransmitters. Child abuse has been strongly correlated with what we call pruning of the neurons, resulting in deficient connections among the myriad of places in the brain. These deficiencies in the neurotransmitters make it impossible for a delusional individual to ever process the feedback that could lead to a challenging of the unrealistic ideas.

Recall that young Nathan was sexually abused by his first governess between the ages of 5 and 10. His second governess was exactly the opposite. She was a punitive, vengeful individual who filled young Nathan's head with images of torture and punishment for impure thoughts.

And what of Richard Loeb? He too developed some very bizarre ideas that he was a master criminal, capable of committing the perfect crime without being detected. He also had an incapacity to experience emotions. He was described as callous and unfeeling, as manipulative, superficial, conning, denying responsibility for his own behavior, and did not have the capacity for remorse or guilt. He lacked any depth to his emotional reactions. None of these characteristics would endear him to other people. If these traits were due to Richard Loeb's own choosing, one could easily dismiss his behavior as evil and unfeeling. However, such is not the case. Richard Loeb, like Nathan Leopold, had a diseased brain. Once again, deficient frontal lobes made it impossible for Loeb to anticipate the consequences of his behavior or to exert the inhibitions and controls over his behavior that most individuals have. And again, brain imaging demonstrates to us the brain impairments, especially in the connections between the frontal lobes and the amygdala, a subcortical organ responsible for emotional control and fear conditioning, and the hippocampus, a part of the brain that processes memory. You have heard our doctors describe Mr. Loeb as a psychopath. Psychopaths have been demonstrated to have deficient connections among the frontal lobes, the amygdala, the hippocampus and the striatal areas. Therefore, an individual such as Mr. Loeb could never learn appropriate fear responses, never know what kinds of behavior were prohibited or, at least, too risky. He is incapable of incorporating corrective memory experiences into his daily functioning because of the deficits in the hippocampus and the frontal lobes.

And what of the interactions between these two disturbed young men? Both had grandiose ideas, one a superman and one the master criminal. Both were incapable of the corrections in perceptions needed by normal individuals to modify the ways in which they handle challenges. Both lacked the capacity for emotional reactions, again for different reasons. However, when these two grossly disordered individuals with significant brain impairment interacted, they created a "perfect storm", a confluence of psychopathology that led to this crime. So, in closing, do not blame these boys. Instead blame the brain deficiencies over which neither Nathan Leopold nor Richard Loeb had any control.

References

Alzheimer's Association. (n.d.). *Early onset dementia: A national challenge, a future crisis*. Retrieved March 1, 2017, from https://www.bing.com/cr?IG=EBBB3ED7EA6B47EAB603C FC6FF88F0DE&CID=2A17AB45028164B7243FA009038765D3&rd=1&h=N9uzFKIc8N72 7dt8HVf1_YtMZ_SZxUYHT9T38NoEa7A&v=1&r=https%3a%2f%2fwww.alz.org%2fnatio nal%2fdocuments%2freport_earlyonset_summary.pdf&p=DevEx,5067.1

American Psychiatric Association. (2013). *Diagnostic and statistical manual of mental disorders* (5th ed.). Arlington, VA: American Psychiatric Publishing.

Baatz, S. (2008). *For the thrill of it: Leopold, Loeb, and the murder that shocked Chicago*. New York, NY: Harper.

Baker-Nigh, A., Vahedi, S., Davis, E. G., Weintraub, S., Bigio, E. H., Klein, W. L., & Geula, C. (2015). Neuronal amyloid-β accumulation within cholinergic basal forebrain in ageing and Alzheimer's disease. *Brain, 138*(6), 1722–1737. https://doi.org/10.1093/brain/awv024

Bell, V., & Halligan, P. W. (2013). The neural basis of abnormal personal belief. In F. Krueger & J. Grafman (Eds.), *The neural basis of human belief systems* (pp. 191–224). New York, NY: Psychology Press.

Boccardi, M., Ganzola, R., Rossi, R., Sabattoli, F., Laakso, M. P., Repo-Tiihonen, E., … Frisoni, G. B. (2010). Abnormal hippocampal shape in offenders with psychopathy. *Human Brain Mapping, 31*(3), 438–447.

Cleckley, H. M. (1941). *The mask of sanity. An attempt to reinterpret the so-called psychopathic personality*. Saint Louis, MO: Mosby.

Corlett, P. R., Taylor, J. R., Wang, X. J., Fletcher, P. C., & Krystal, J. H. (2010). Toward a neurobiology of delusions. *Progress in Neurobiology, 92*(3), 345–369.

Decety, J., & Moriguchi, Y. (2007). The empathic brain and its dysfunction in psychiatric populations: Implications for intervention across different clinical conditions. *Biopsychosocial Medicine, 1*(1), 22.

Darrow, C. S., & Dershowitz, A. M. (1996). *The story of my life*. USA: Da Capo Press.

Fujii, D. E. M., Ahmed, I., & Takeshita, J. (1999). Neuropsychologic implications in erotomania: Two case studies. *Neuropsychiatry, Neuropsychology, & Behavioral Neurology, 12*(2), 110–116.

Graham v. Florida, 560 U.S. 48. (2010).

Hare, R. D. (1991). *The Hare psychopathy checklist-revised: Manual*. Toronto, ON: Multi-Health Systems.

Hecht, B. (1966). *Gaily, gaily*. London: New English Library.

Higdon, H. (1999). *Leopold and Loeb: The crime of the century*. Urbana, IL: University of Illinois Press.

Hitchcock, A. (Director), & Hitchcock, A. (Producer). (1948). *Rope [Motion picture]*. United States: Warner Brothers.

Kunert, H. J., Norra, C., & Hoff, P. (2007). Theories of delusional disorders. *Psychopathology, 40*(3), 191–202.

© Springer International Publishing AG 2018   57
D. L. Shapiro et al., *Retrying Leopold and Loeb*, SpringerBriefs in Psychology,
https://doi.org/10.1007/978-3-319-74600-5

Levin, M. (1956). *Compulsion*. New York: Simon and Schuster.

Miller v. Alabama, 567 U.S. 460. (2012).

Mutluer, T., Şar, V., Kose-Demiray, Ç., Arslan, H., Tamer, S., Inal, S., & Kaçar, A. Ş. (2017). Lateralization of neurobiological response in adolescents with post-traumatic stress disorder related to severe childhood sexual abuse: The Tri-Modal Reaction (T-MR) model of protection. *Journal of Trauma & Dissociation,* 1–18. doi:10.1080/15299732.2017.1304489

Morimoto, K., Miyatake, R., Nakamura, M., Watanabe, T., Hirao, T., & Suwaki, H. (2002). Delusional disorder: Molecular genetic evidence for dopamine psychosis. *Neuropsychopharmacology, 26*(6), 794–801.

Nietzsche, F. W., & Kaufmann, W. A. (1995). *Thus spoke Zarathustra: A book for all and none.* New York, NY: Modern Library.

Puente, A. E., & Tonkonogy, J. M. (2009). *Localization of clinical syndromes in neuropsychology and neuroscience.* New York, NY: Springer.

Raine, A. (1993). *The psychopathology of crime: Criminal behavior as a clinical disorder.* San Diego, CA: Academic Press.

Raine, A. (2014). *The anatomy of violence: The biological roots of crime.* London: Penguin Books.

Roper v. Simmons 543 U.S. 551. (2005).

Strozier. (2004, February). *Neurobiological trauma.* Paper presented at meeting of APA Division 43, Fort Lauderdale, Florida.

Printed by Printforce, the Netherlands